I0507204

Unicorn Coloring Book for kids ages 7-11

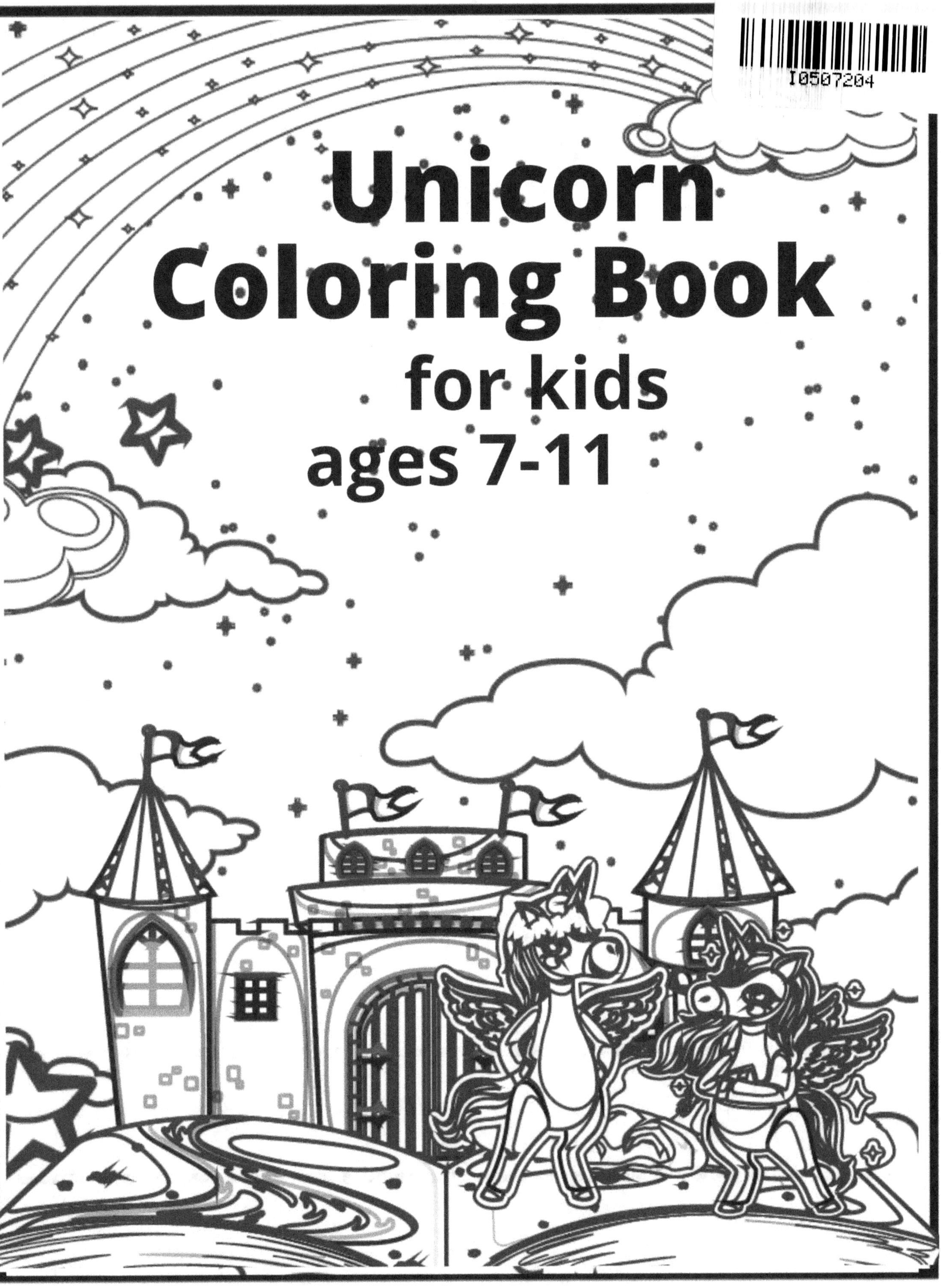

THIS BOOK BELONGS TO

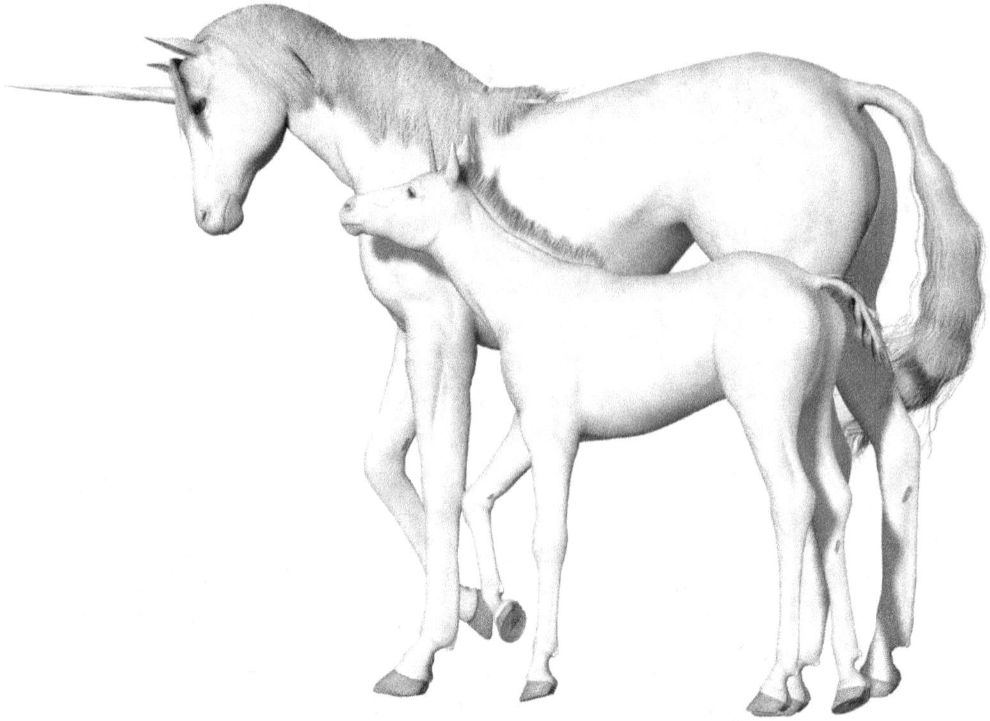

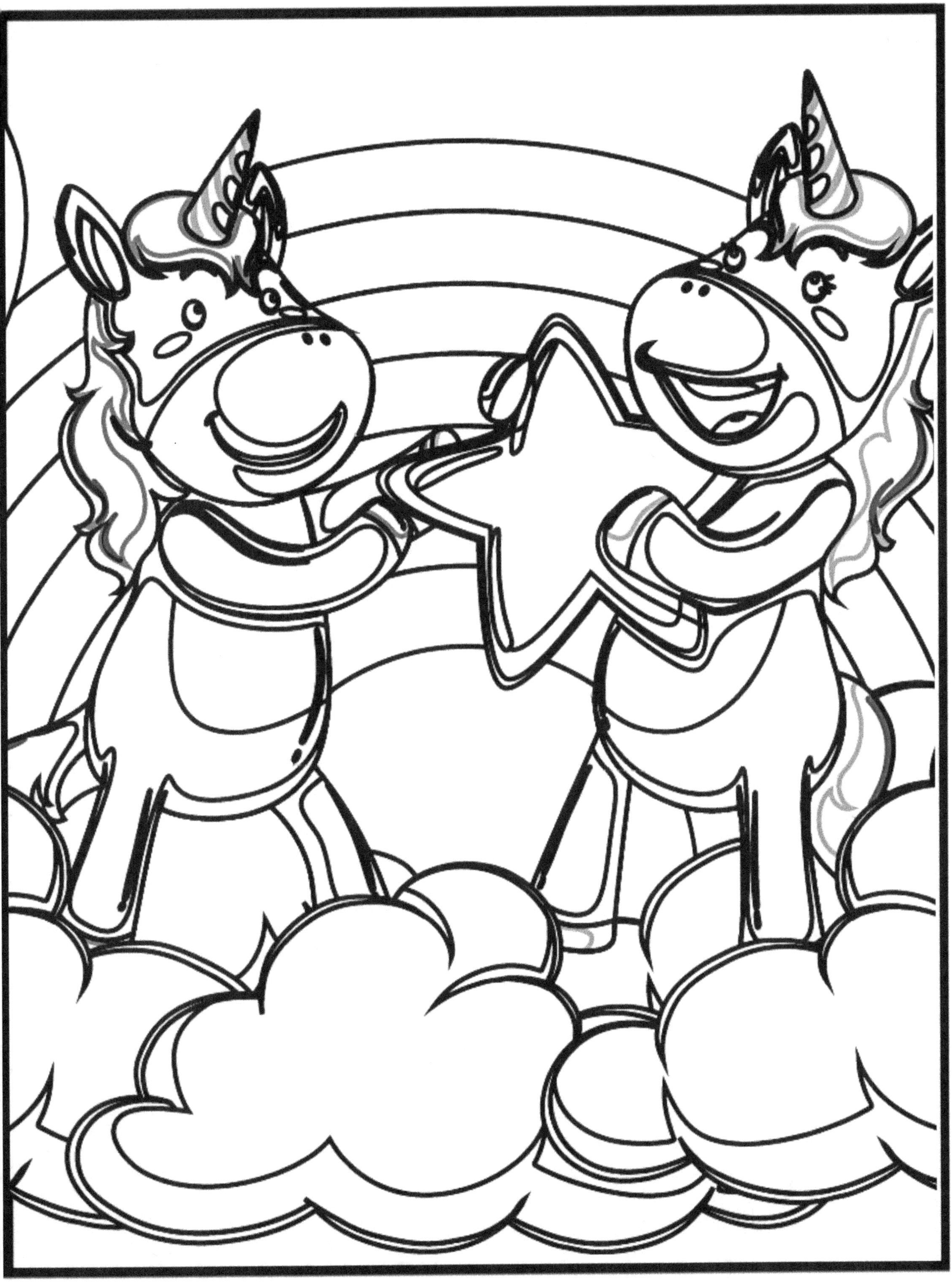

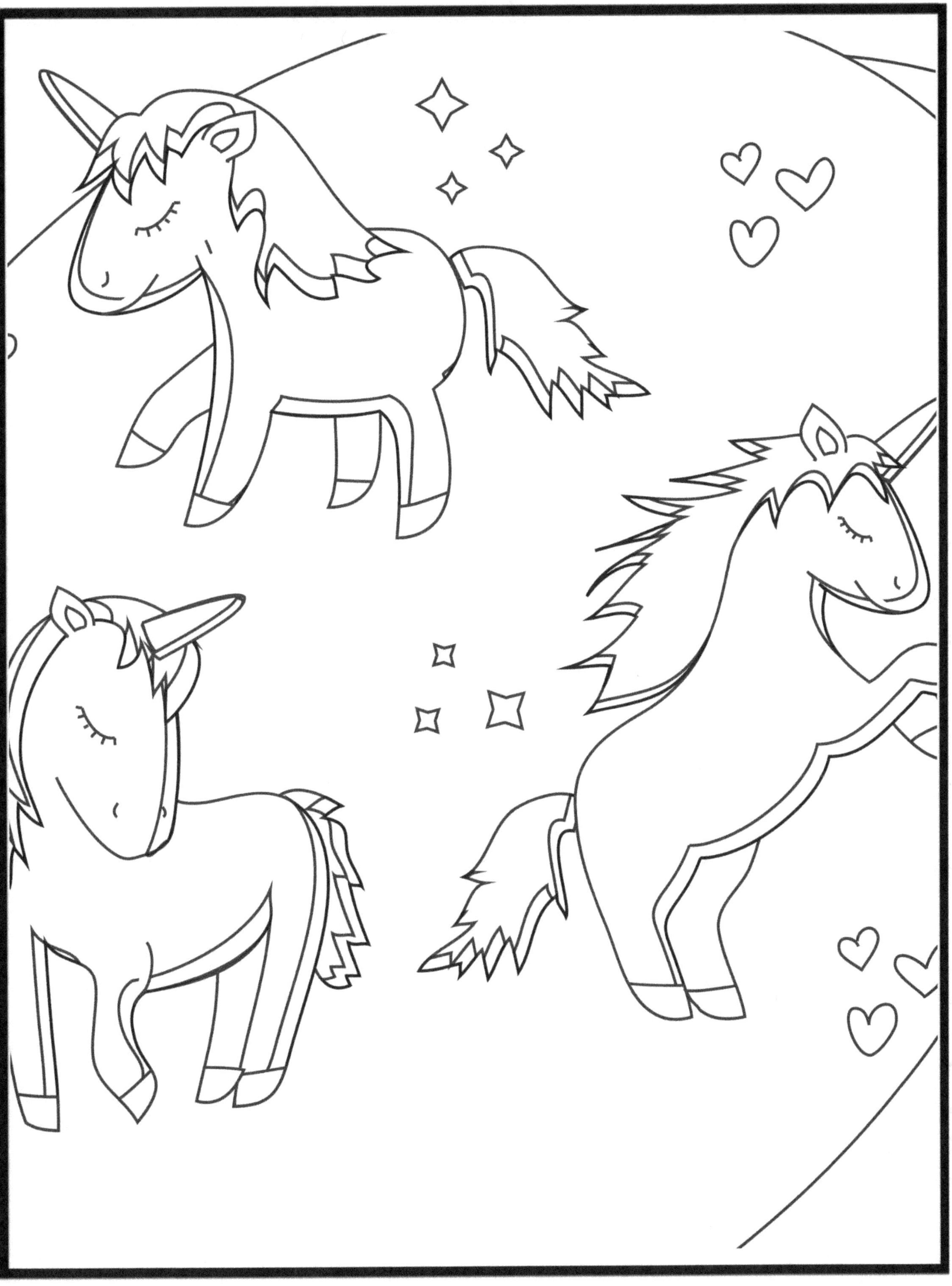

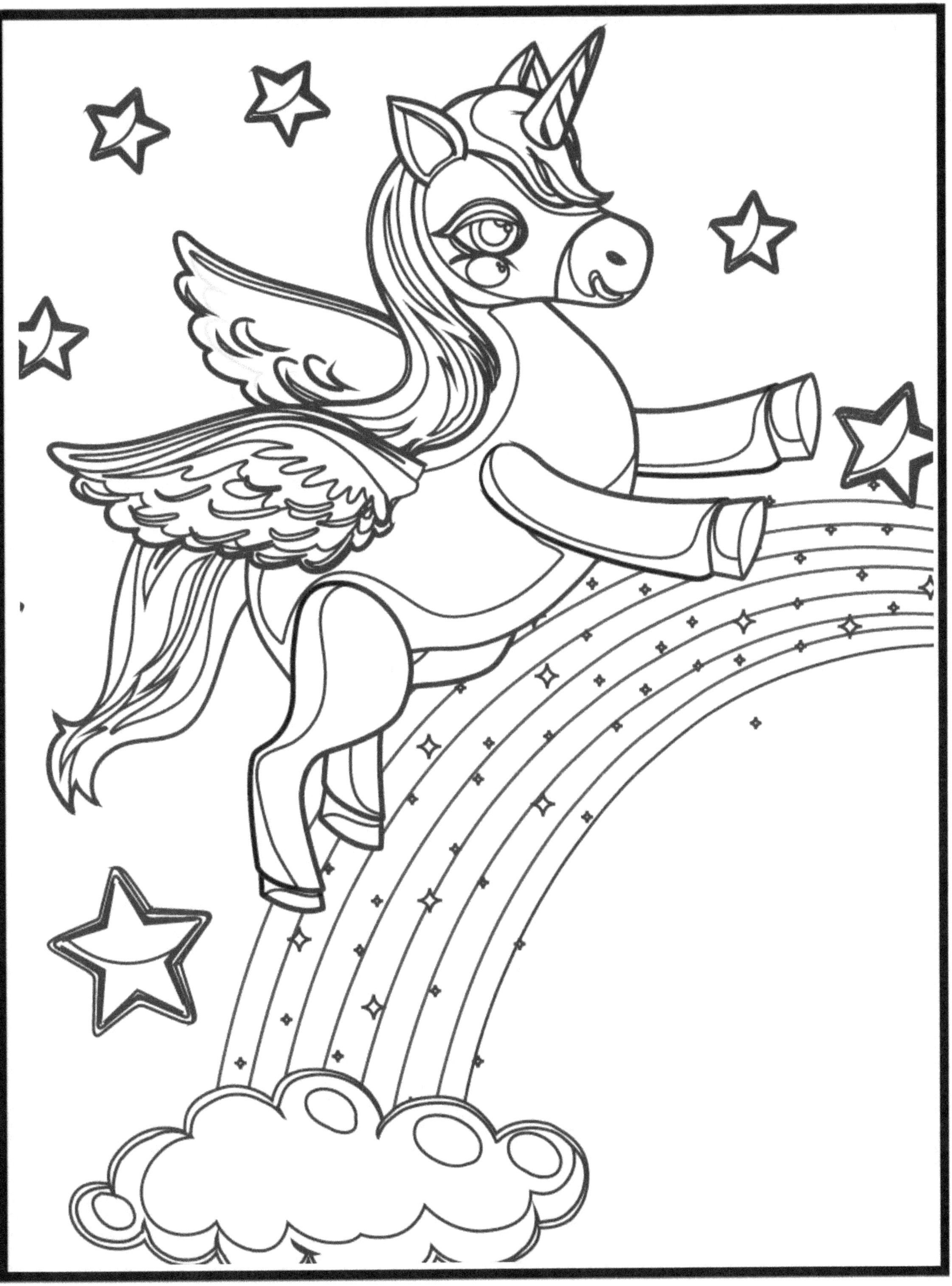

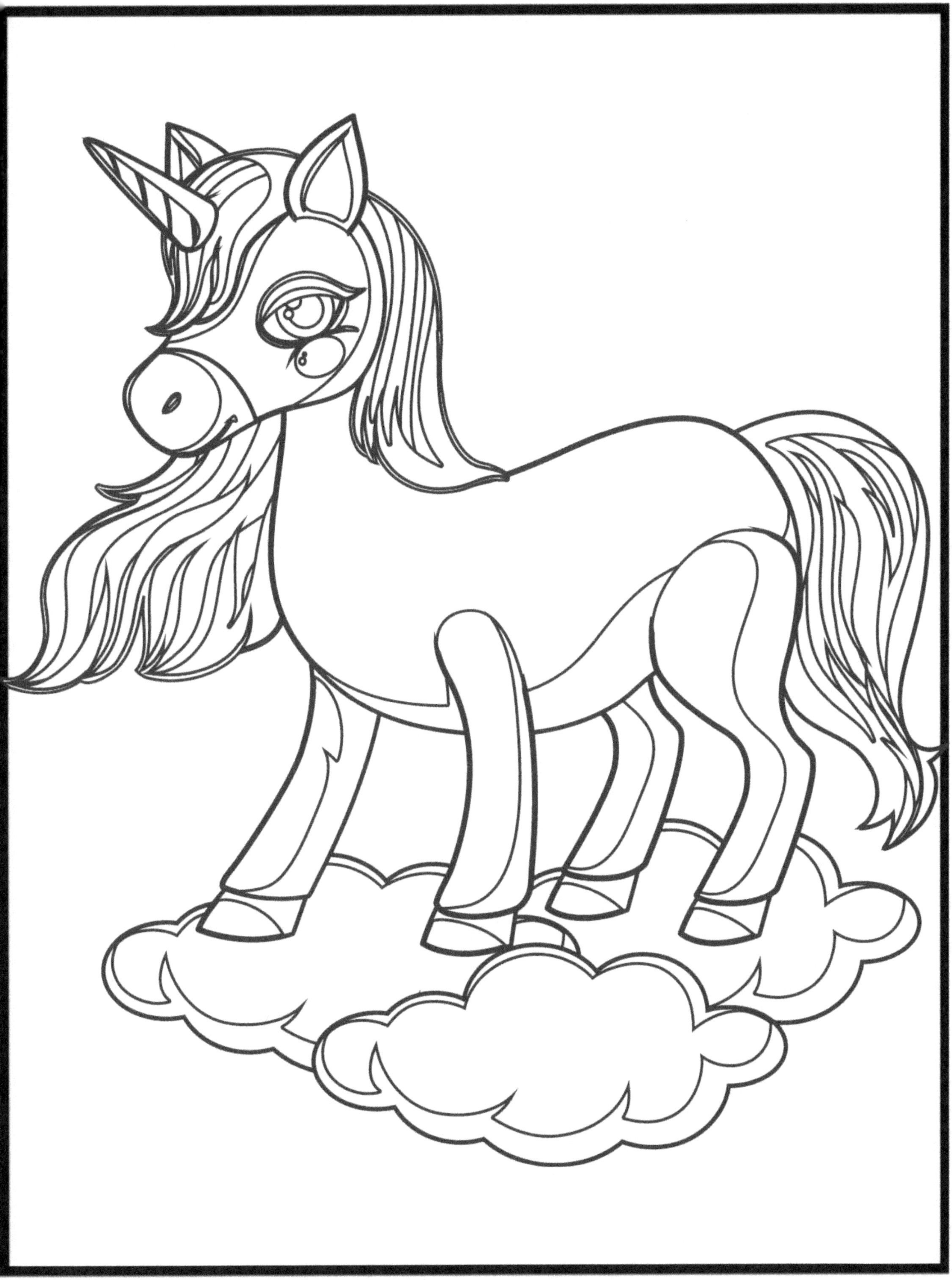

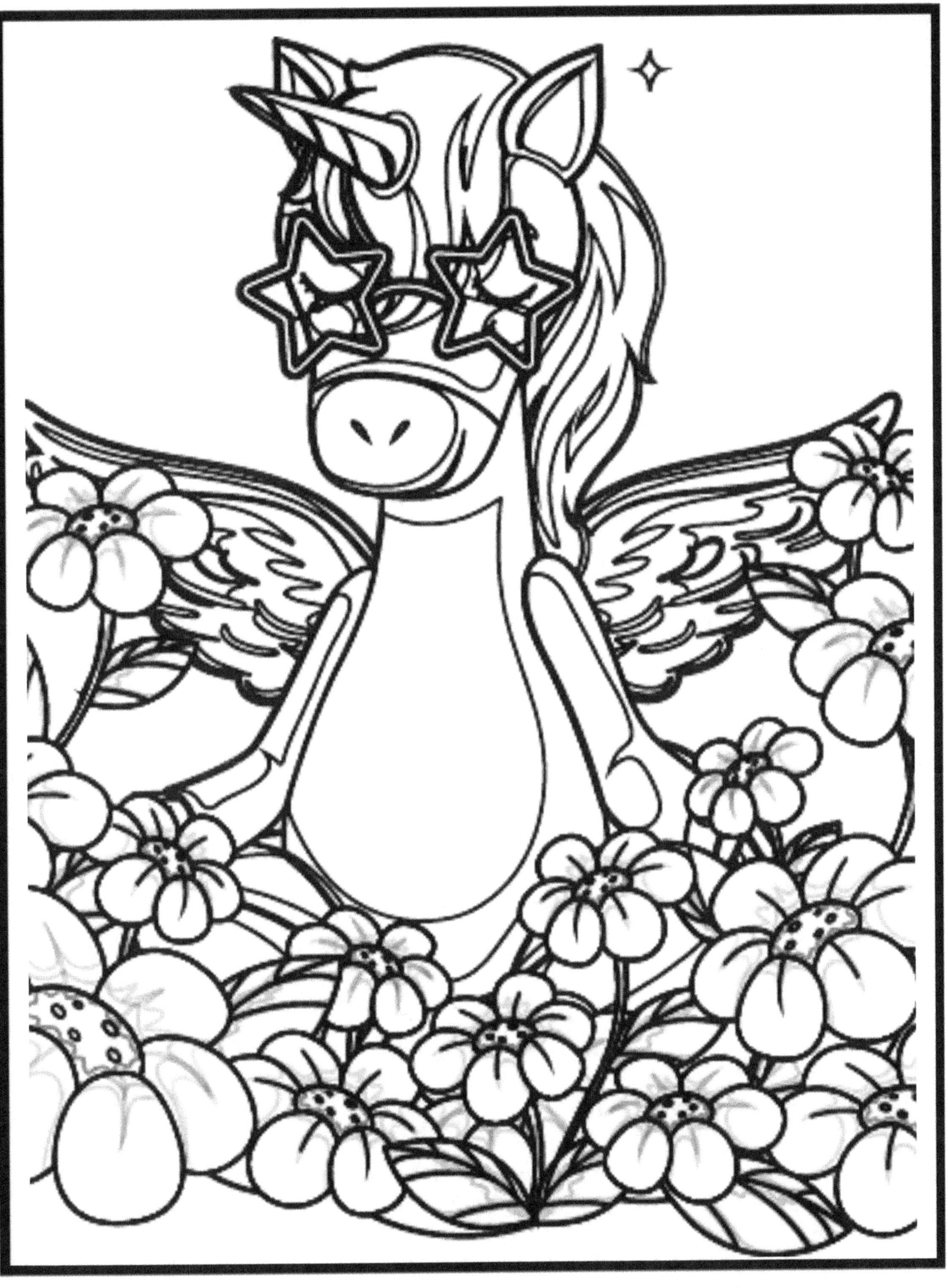

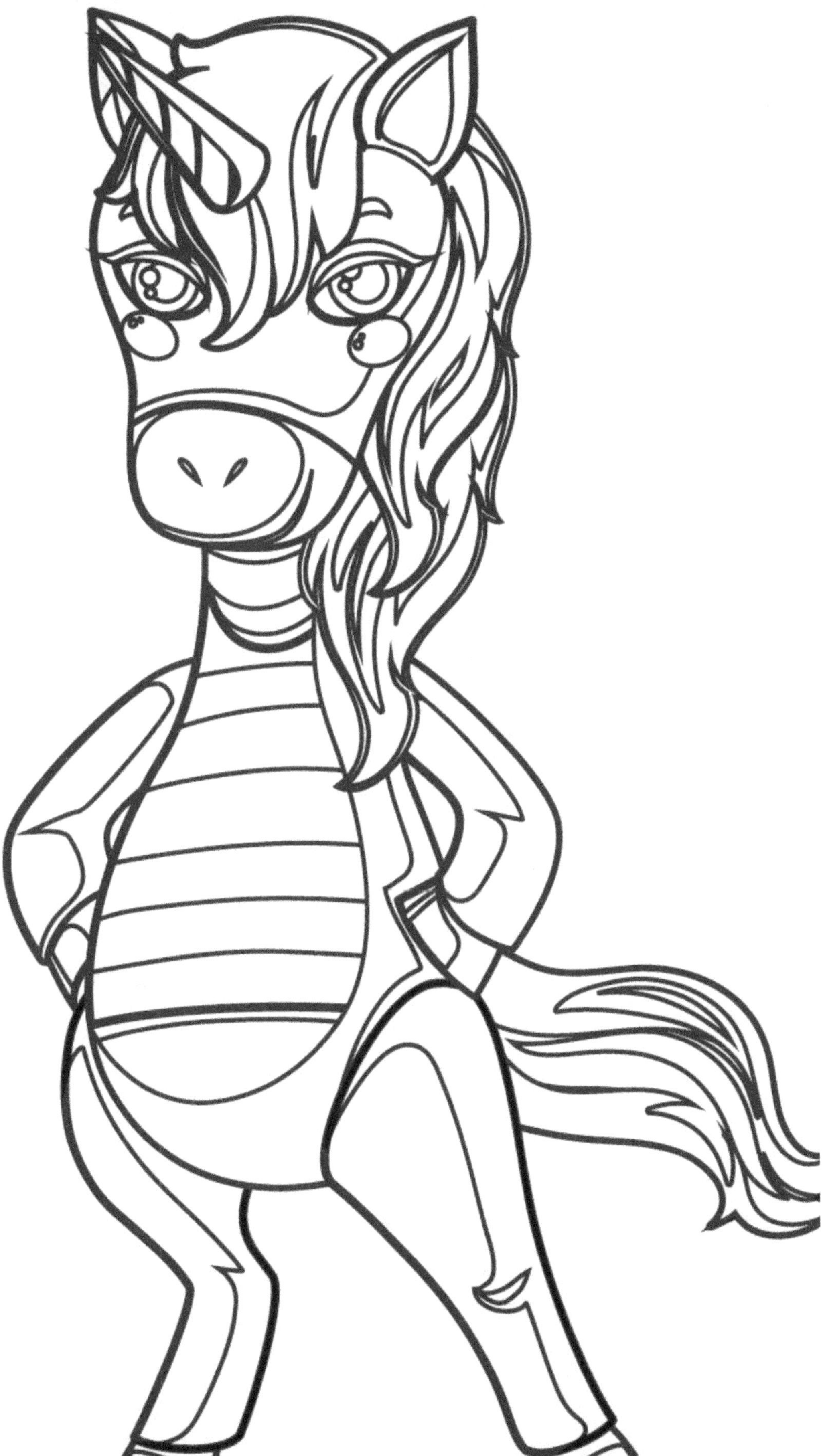

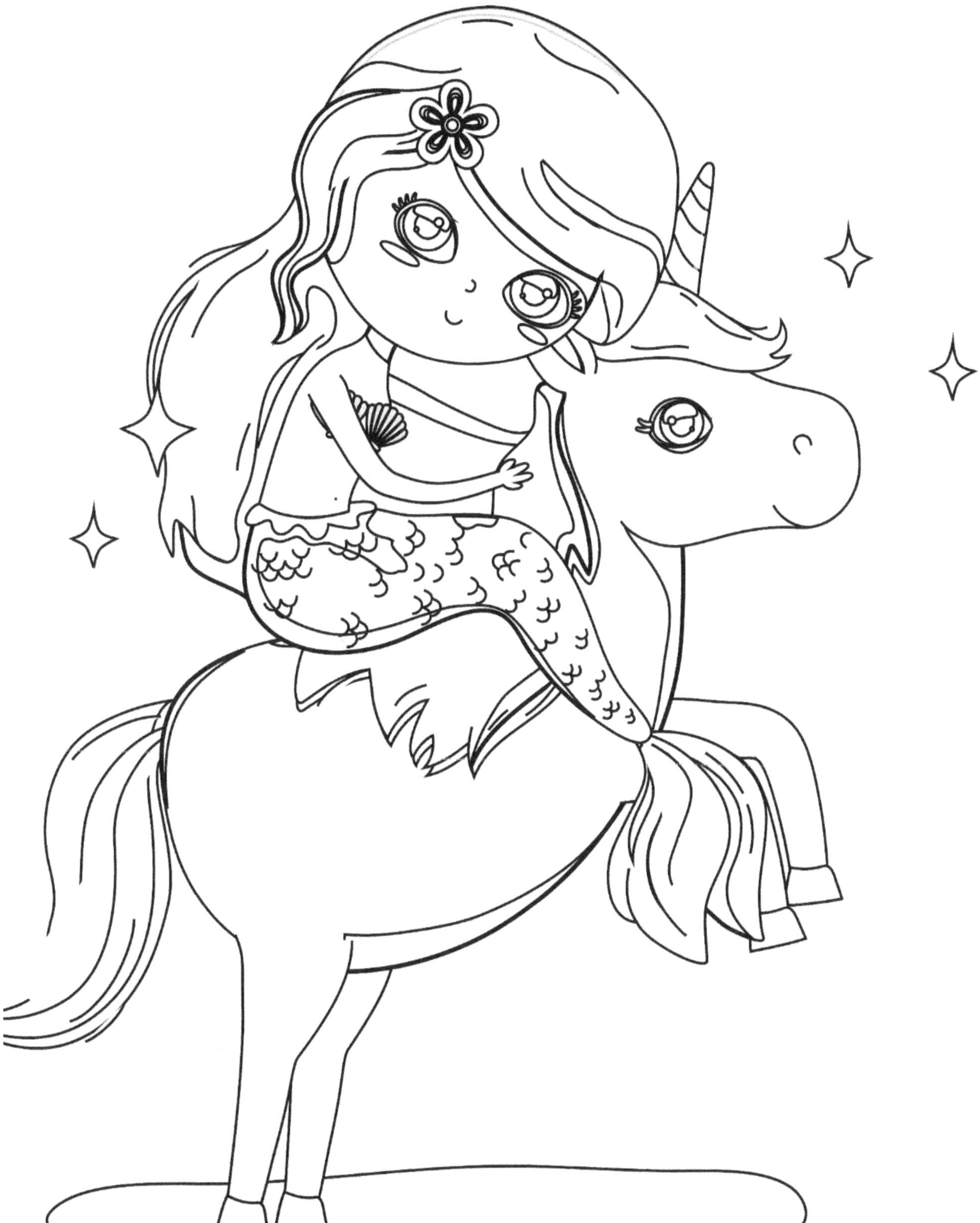

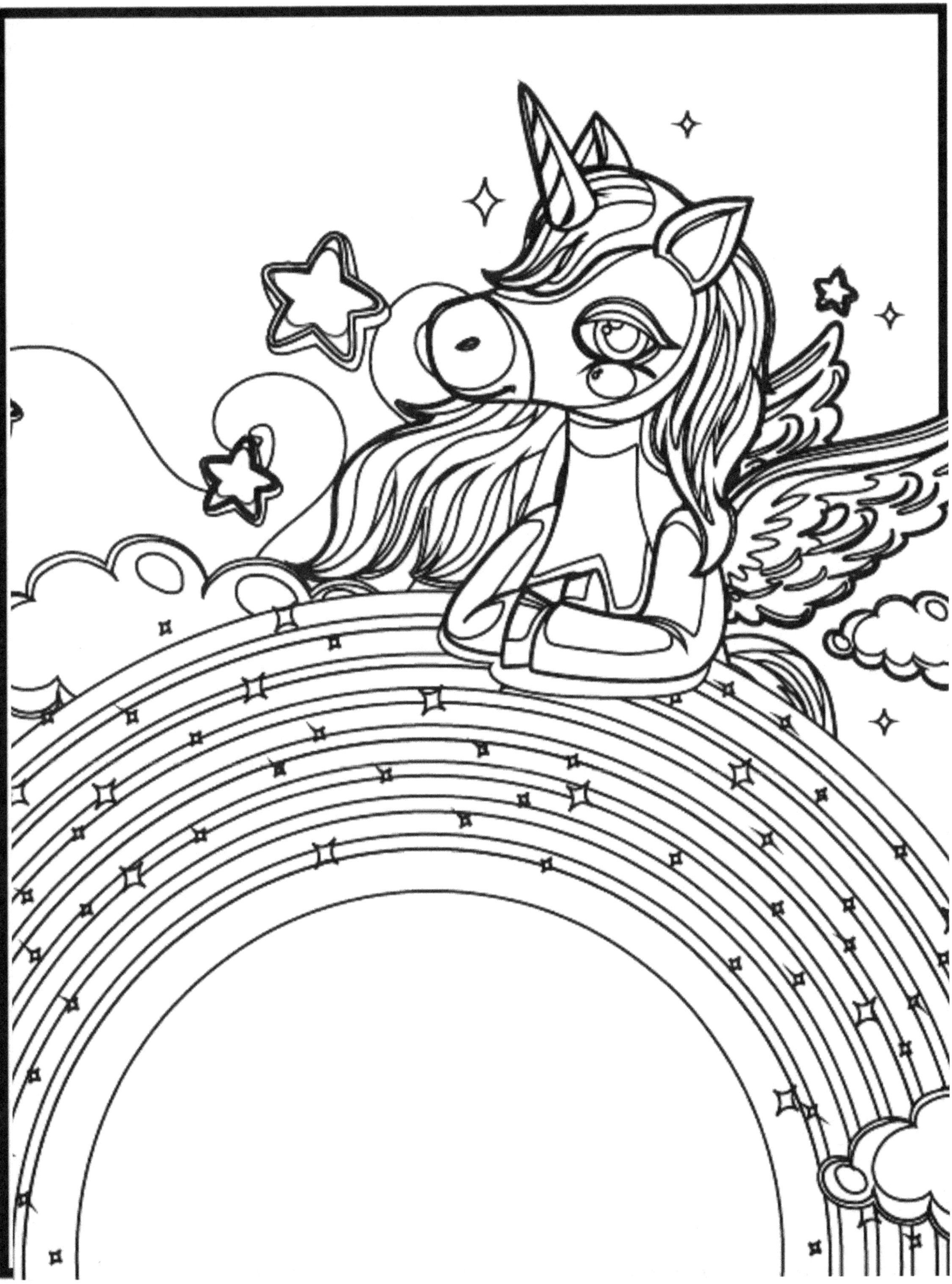

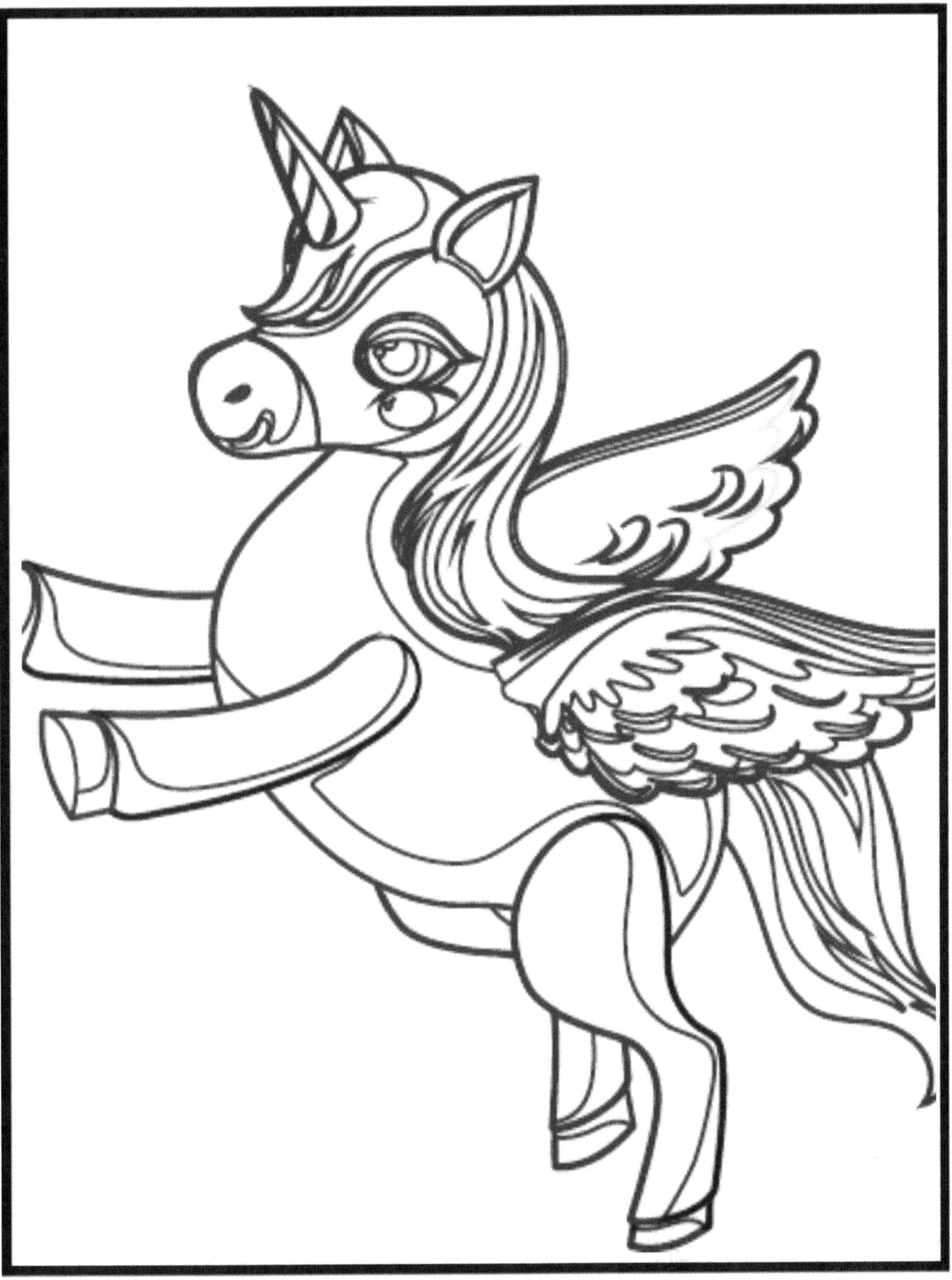

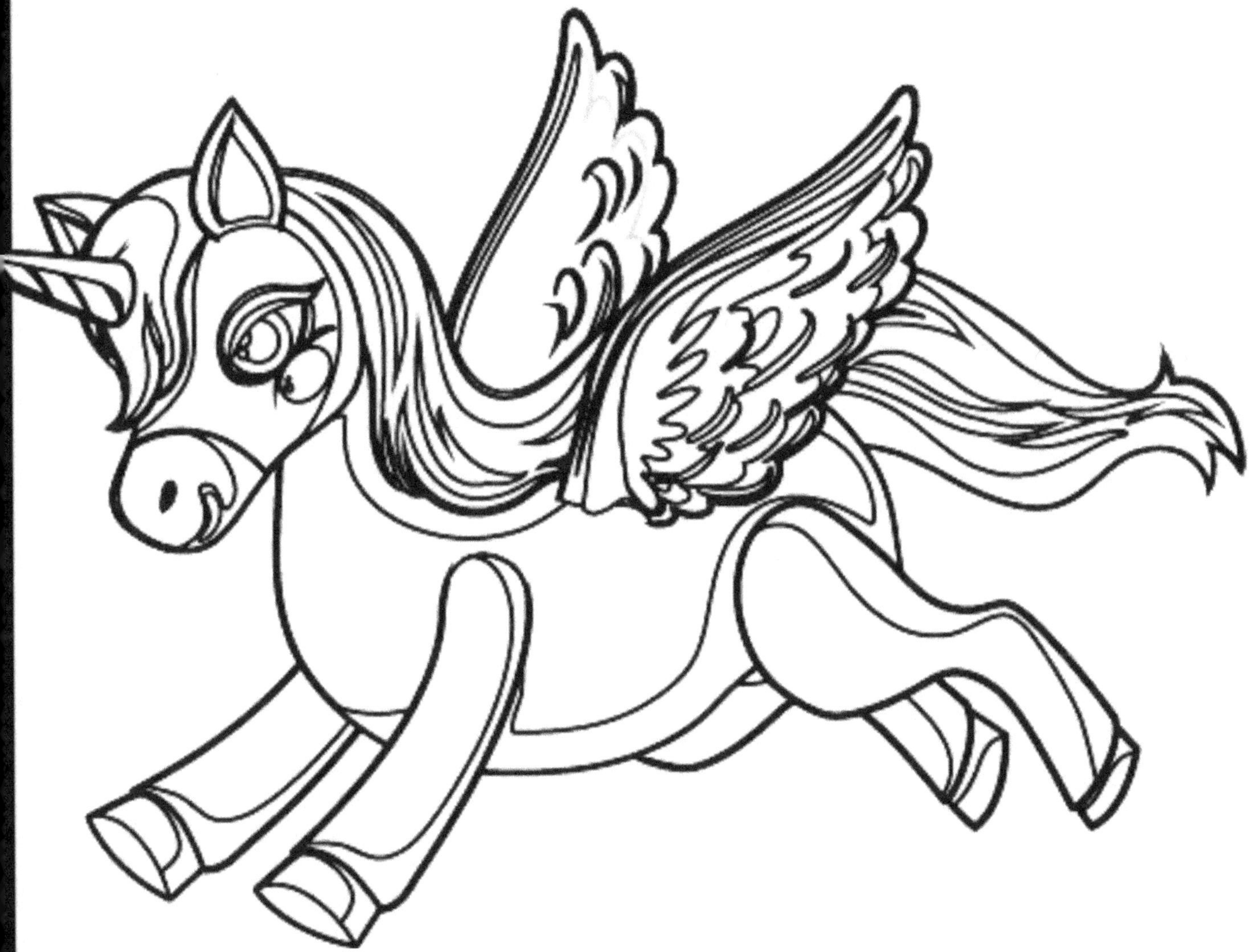

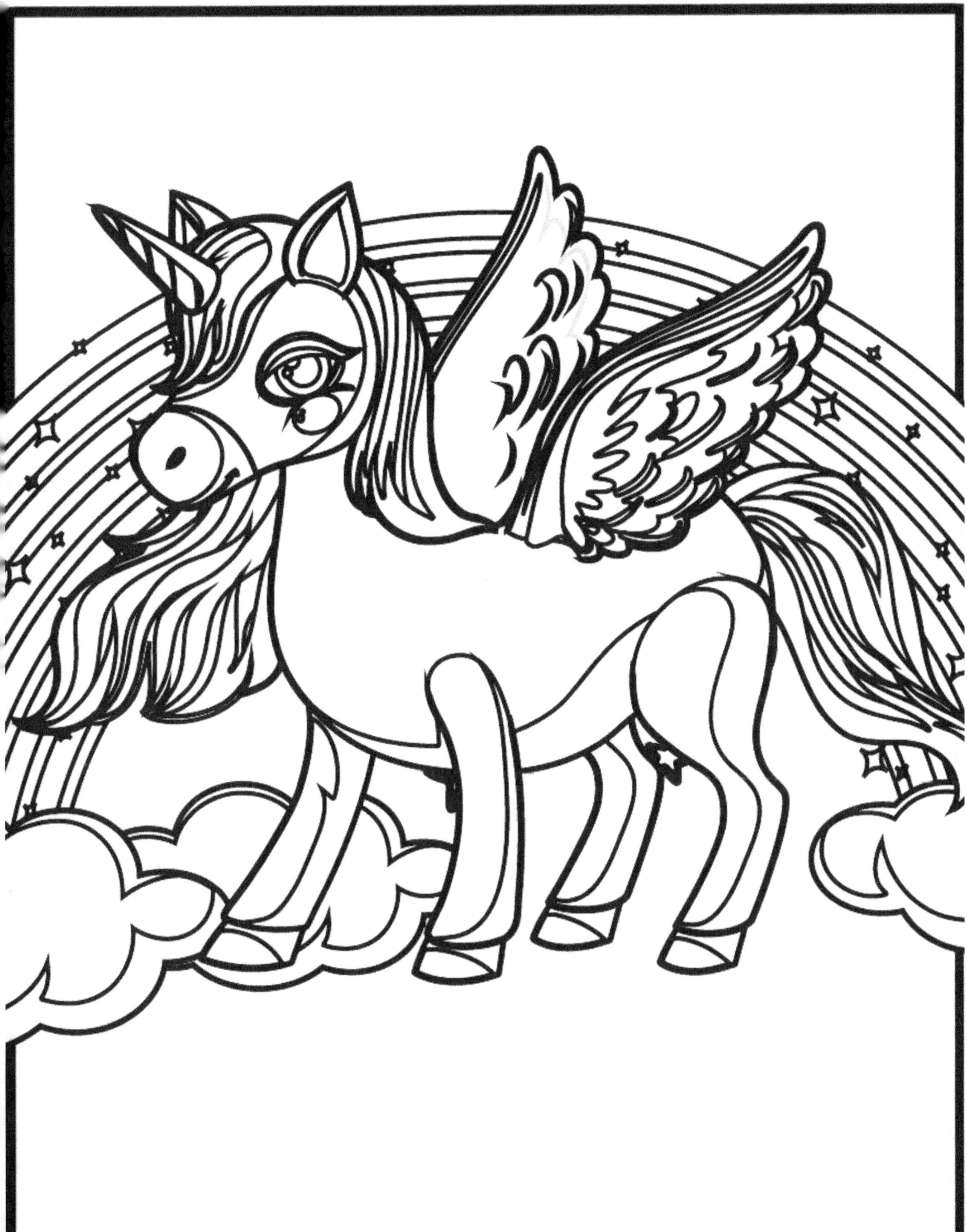

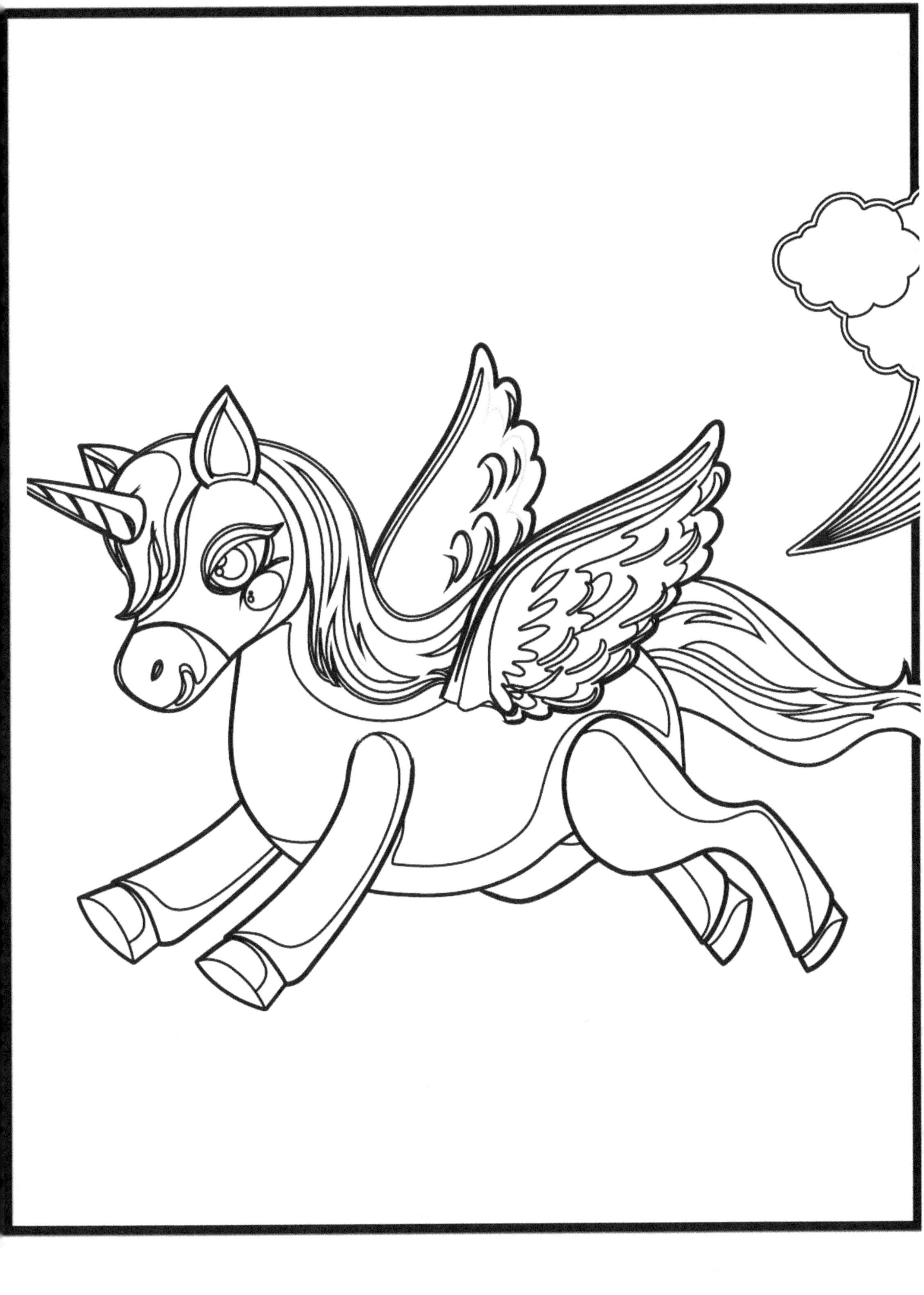

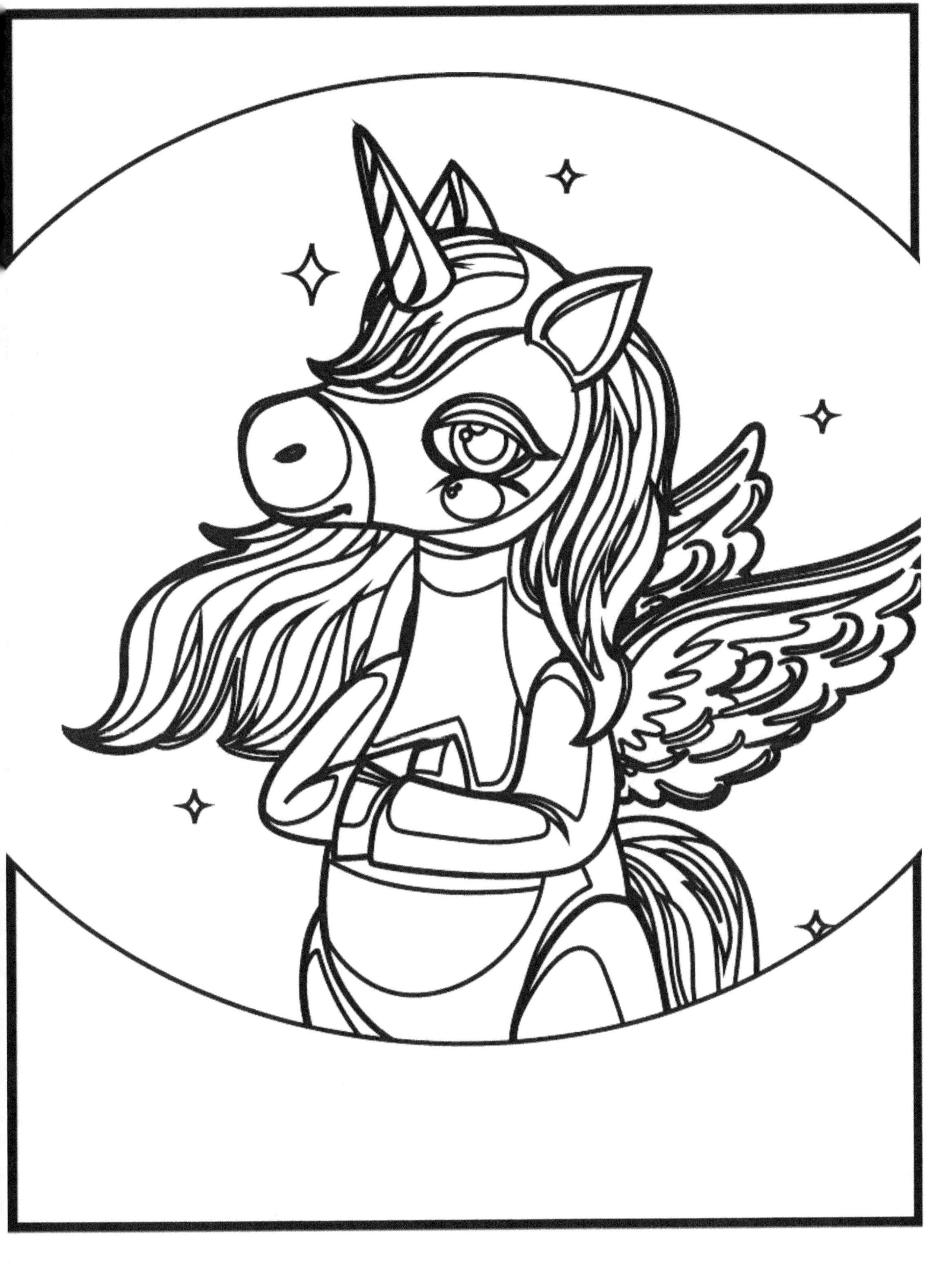

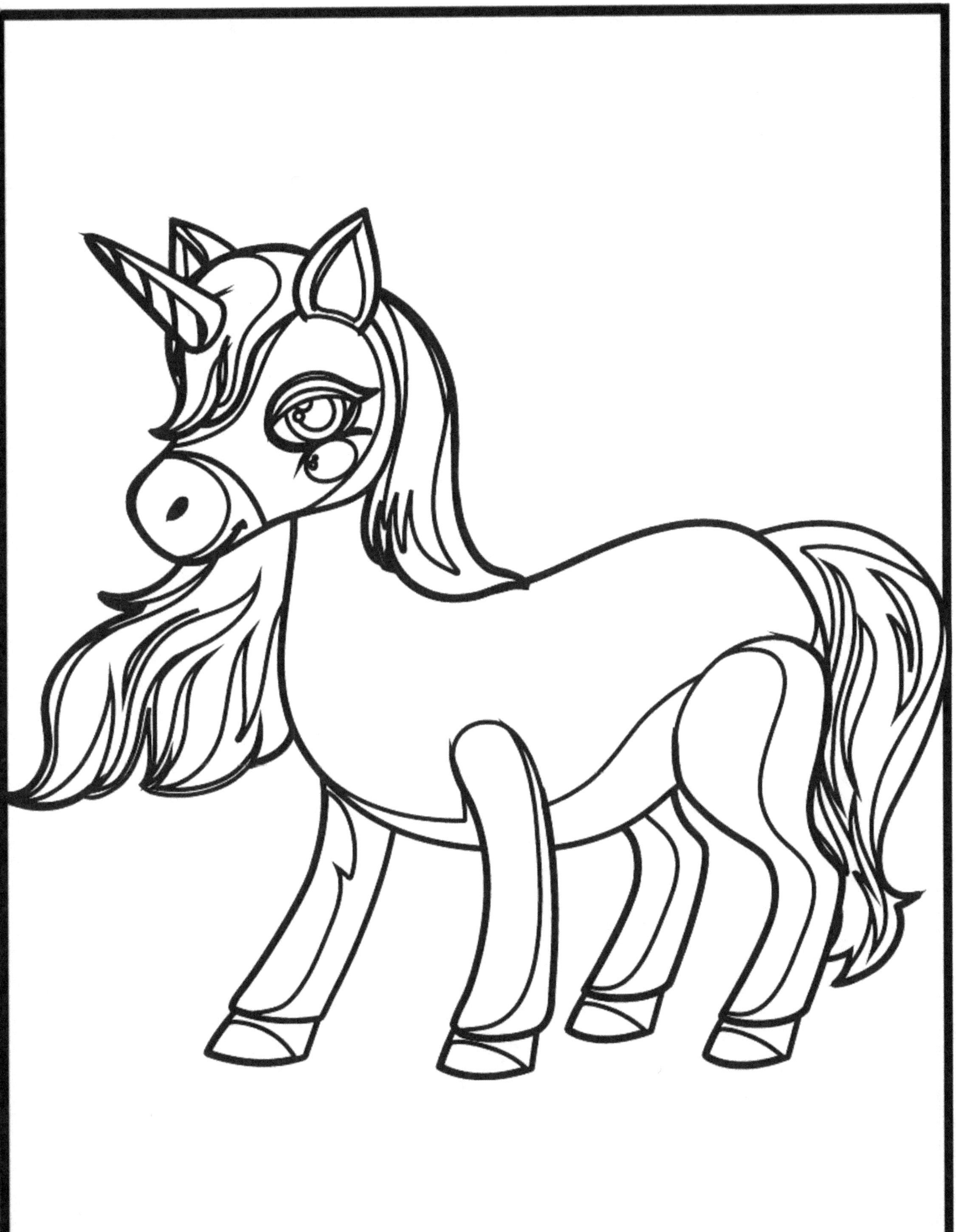

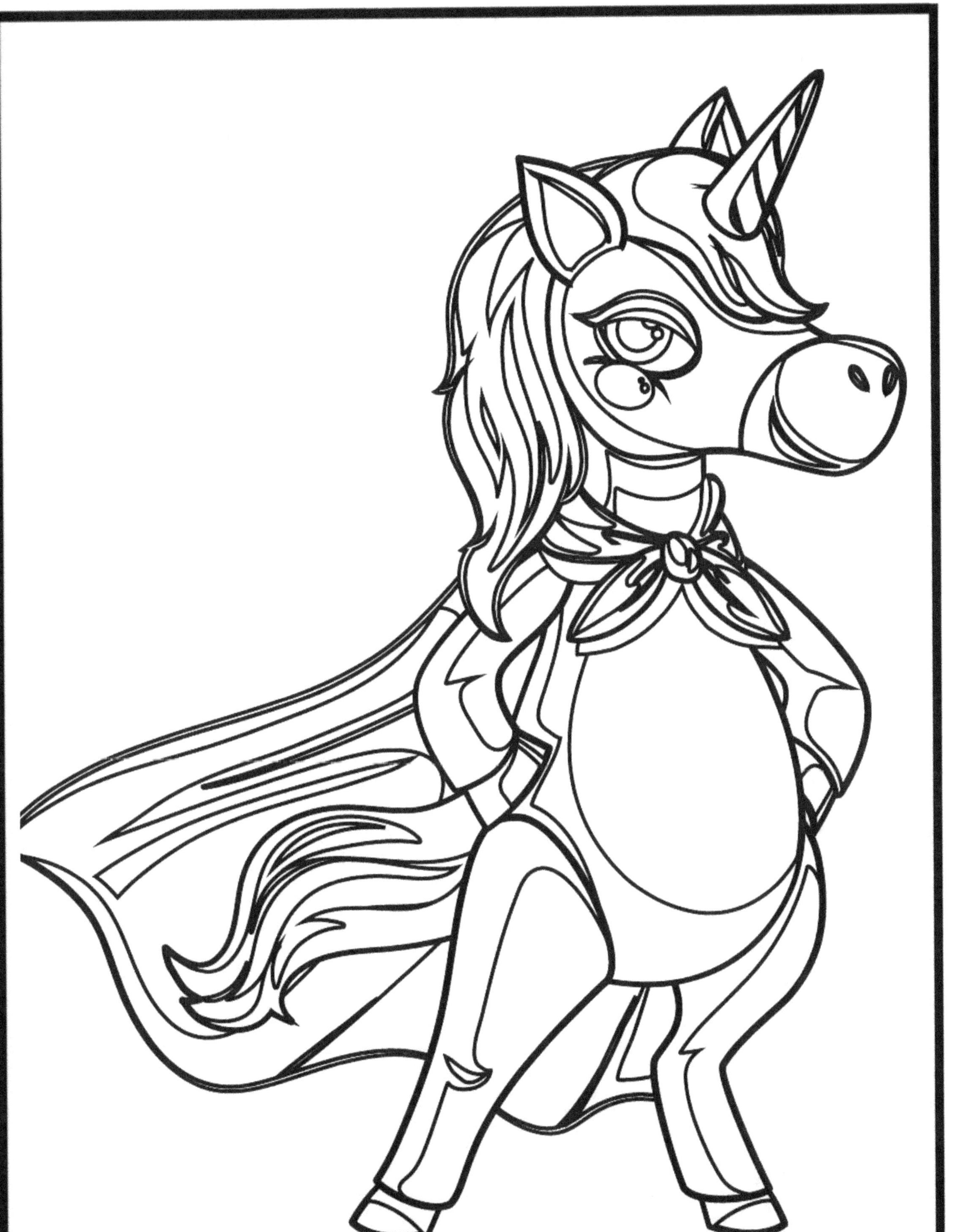

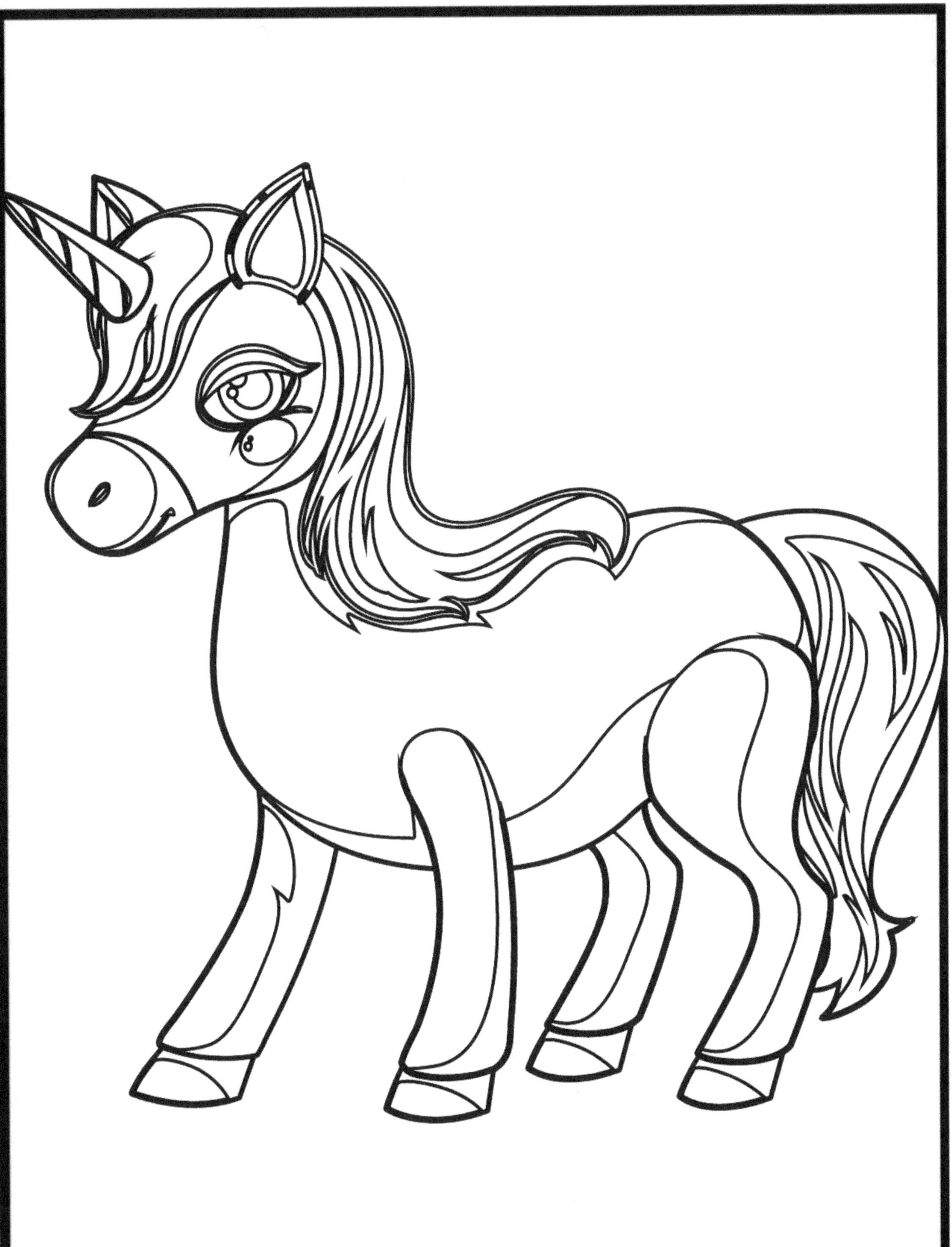

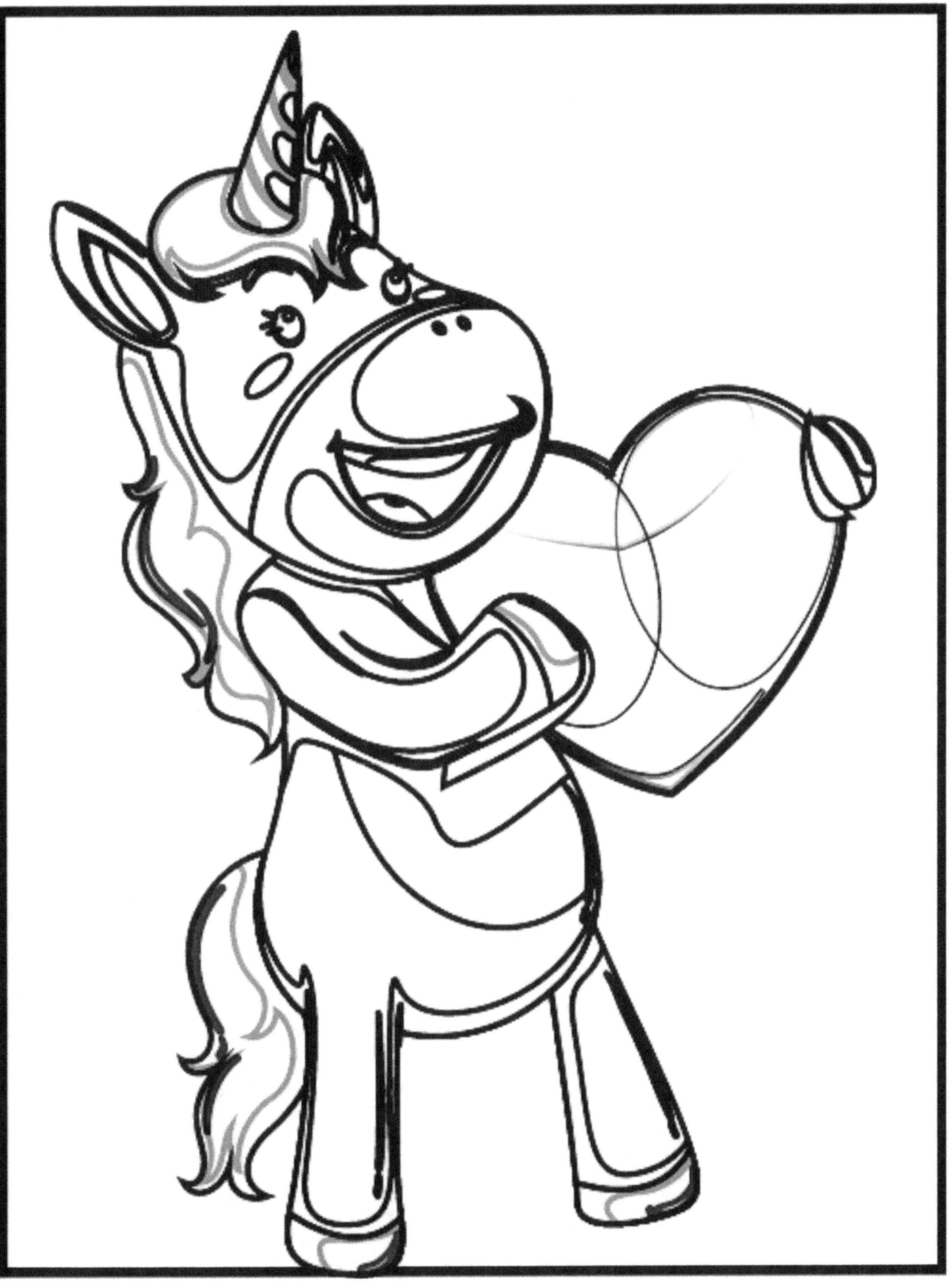

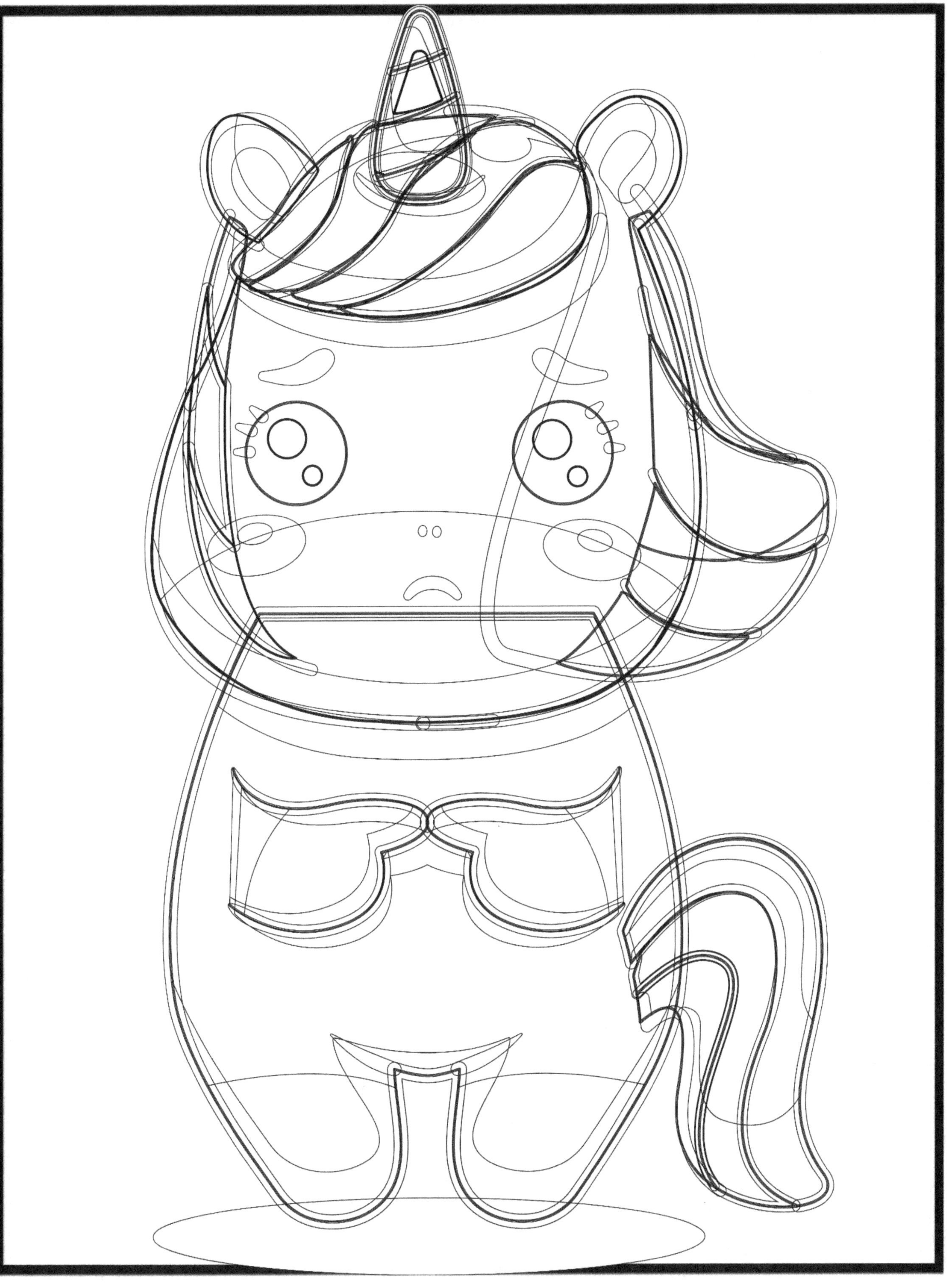

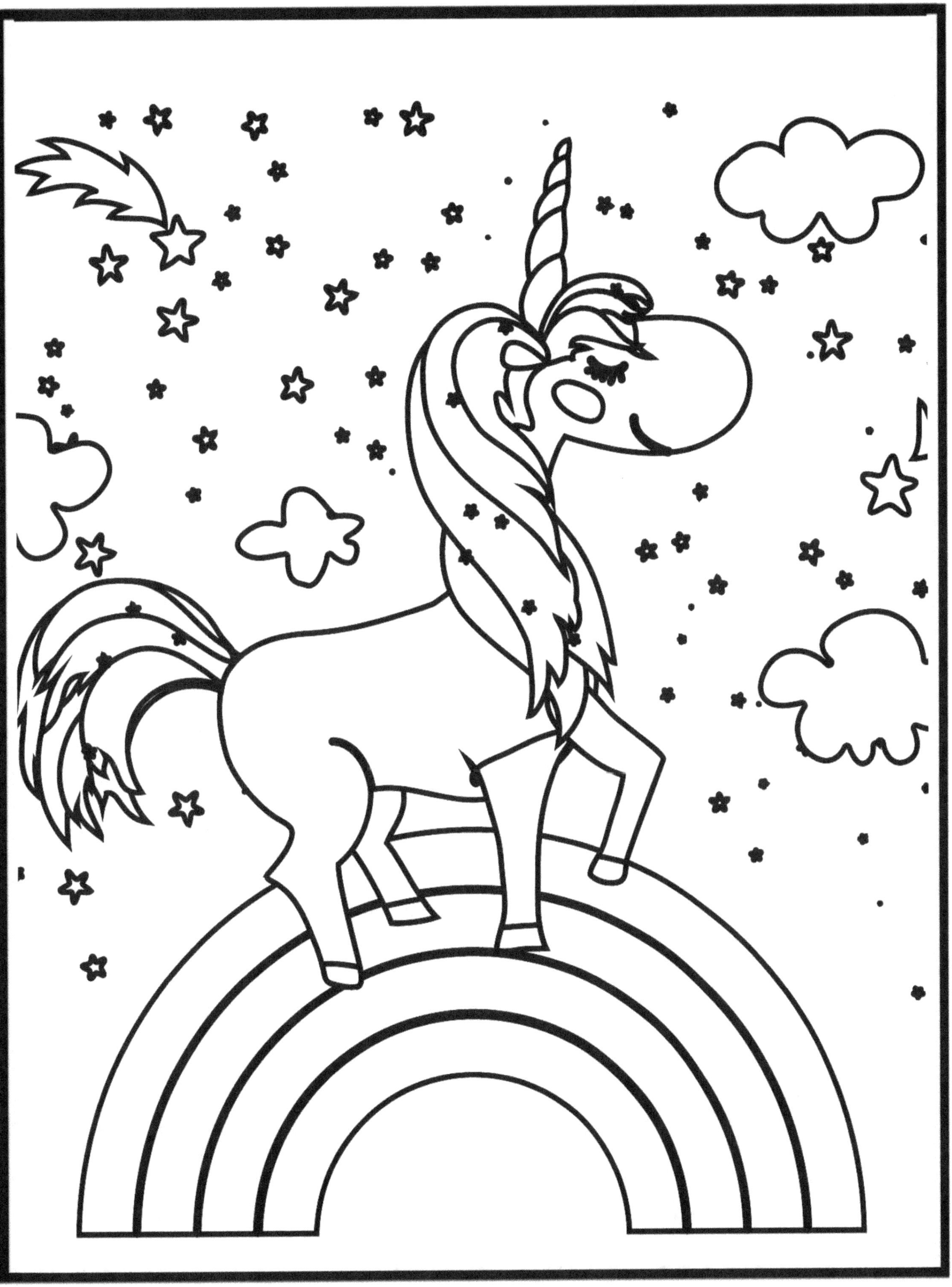

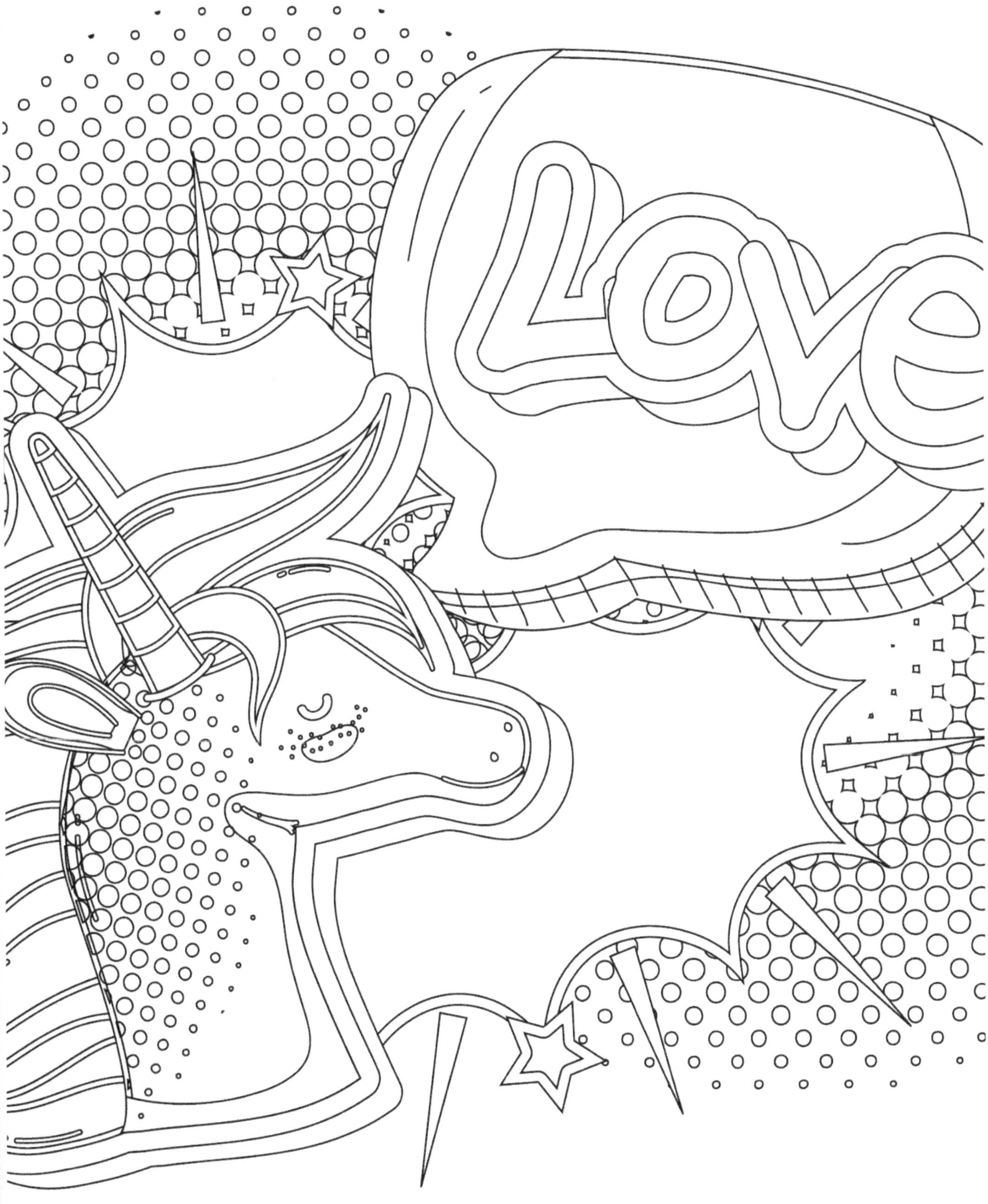
Love

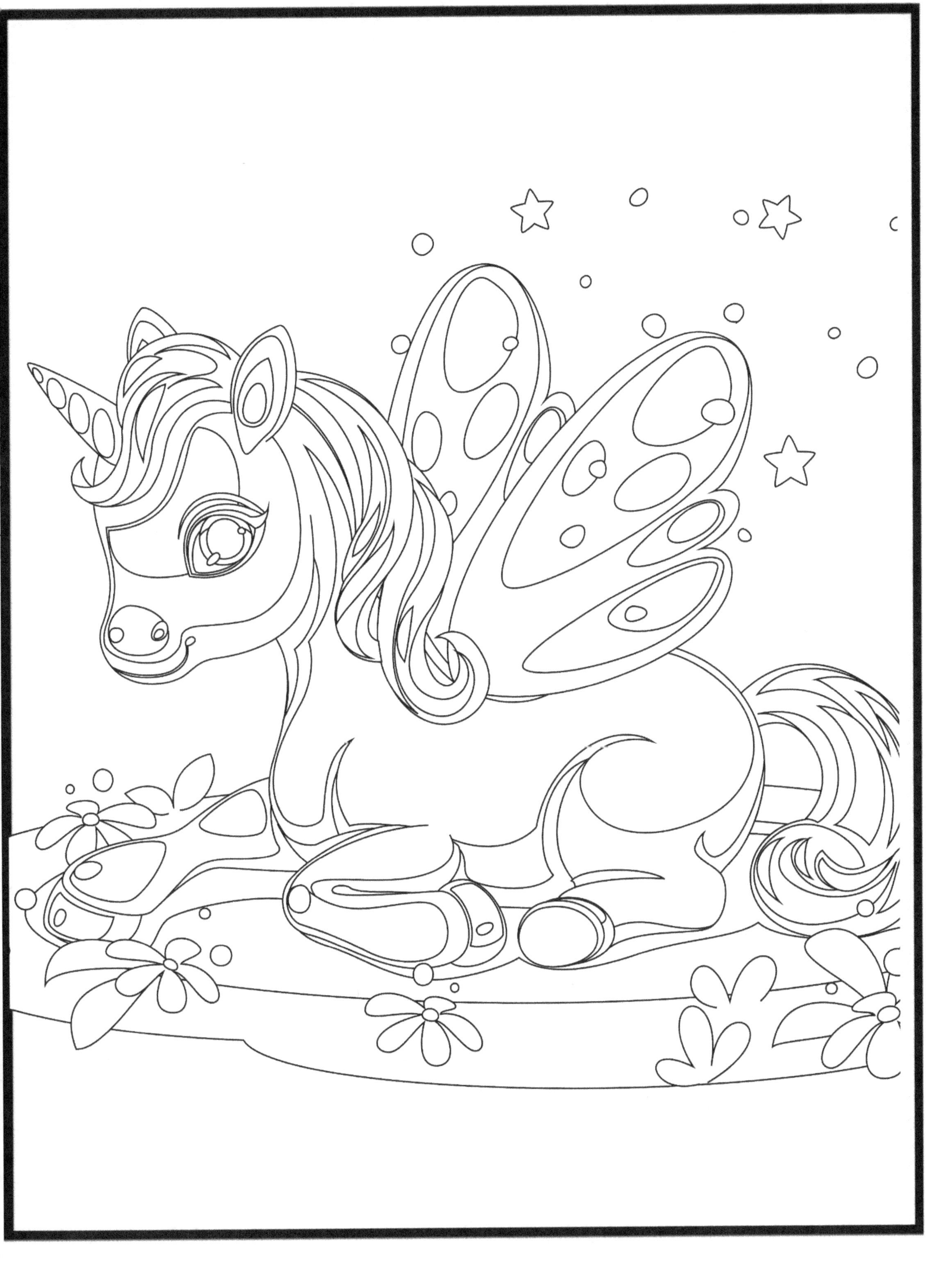

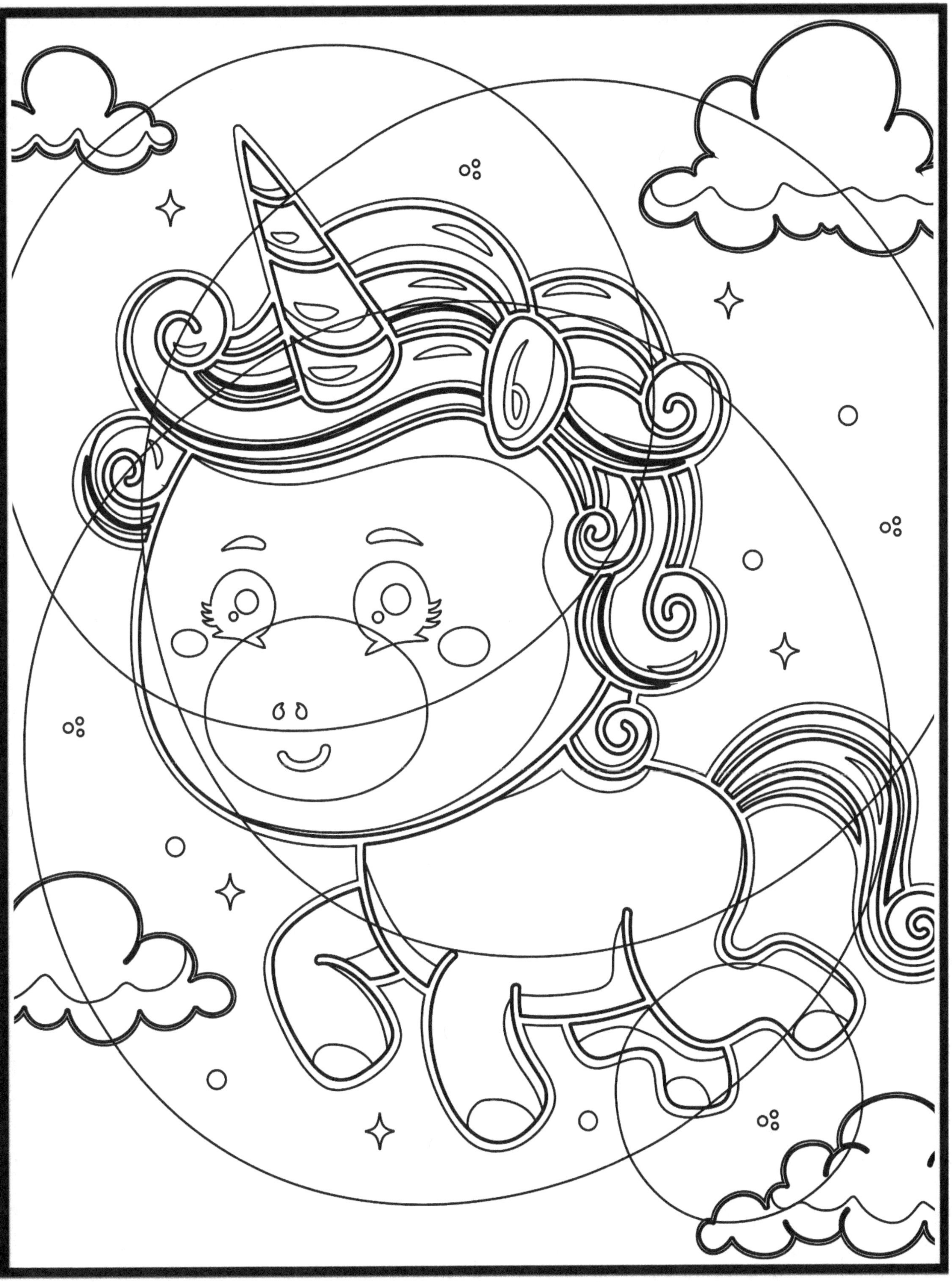

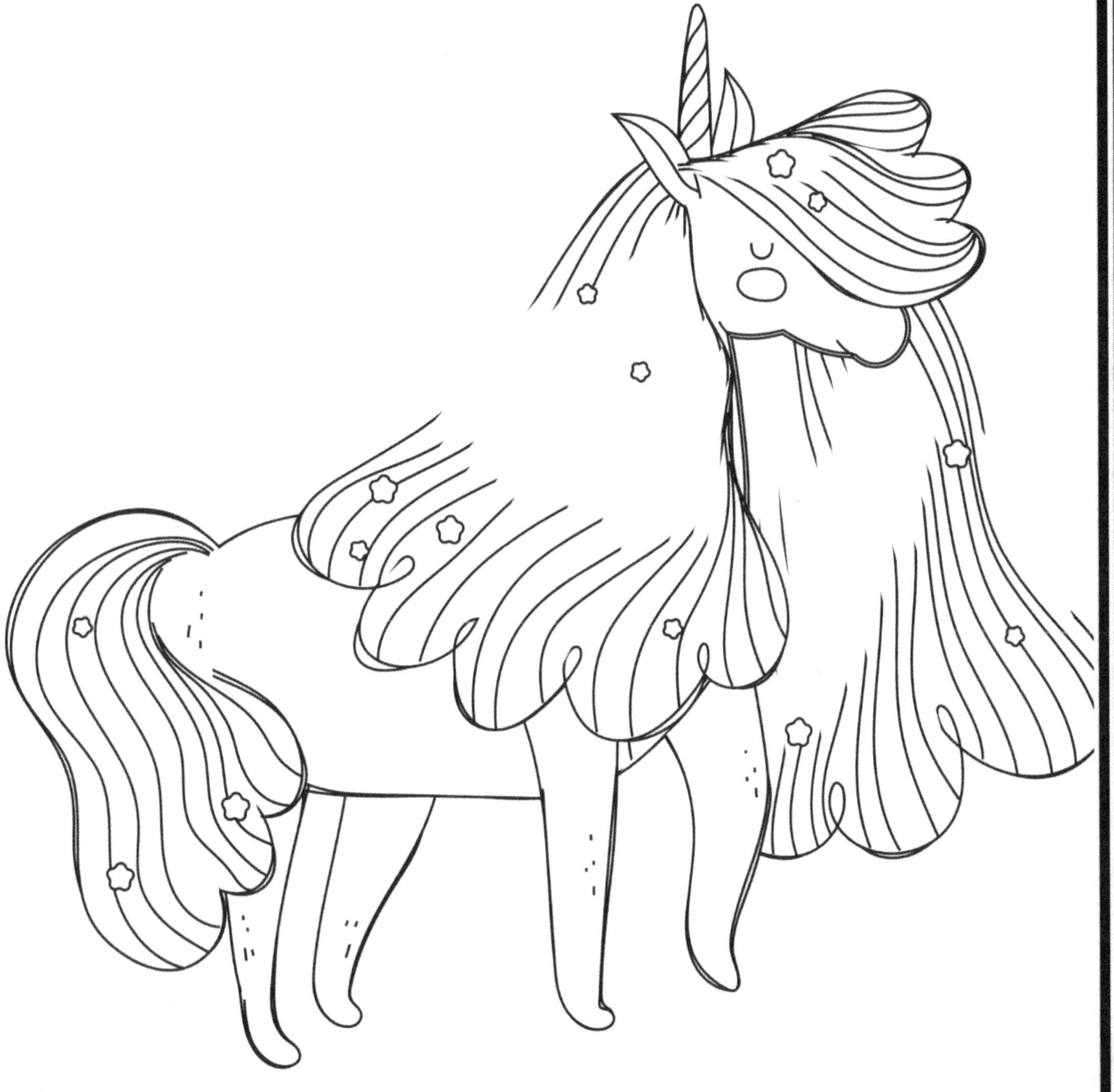

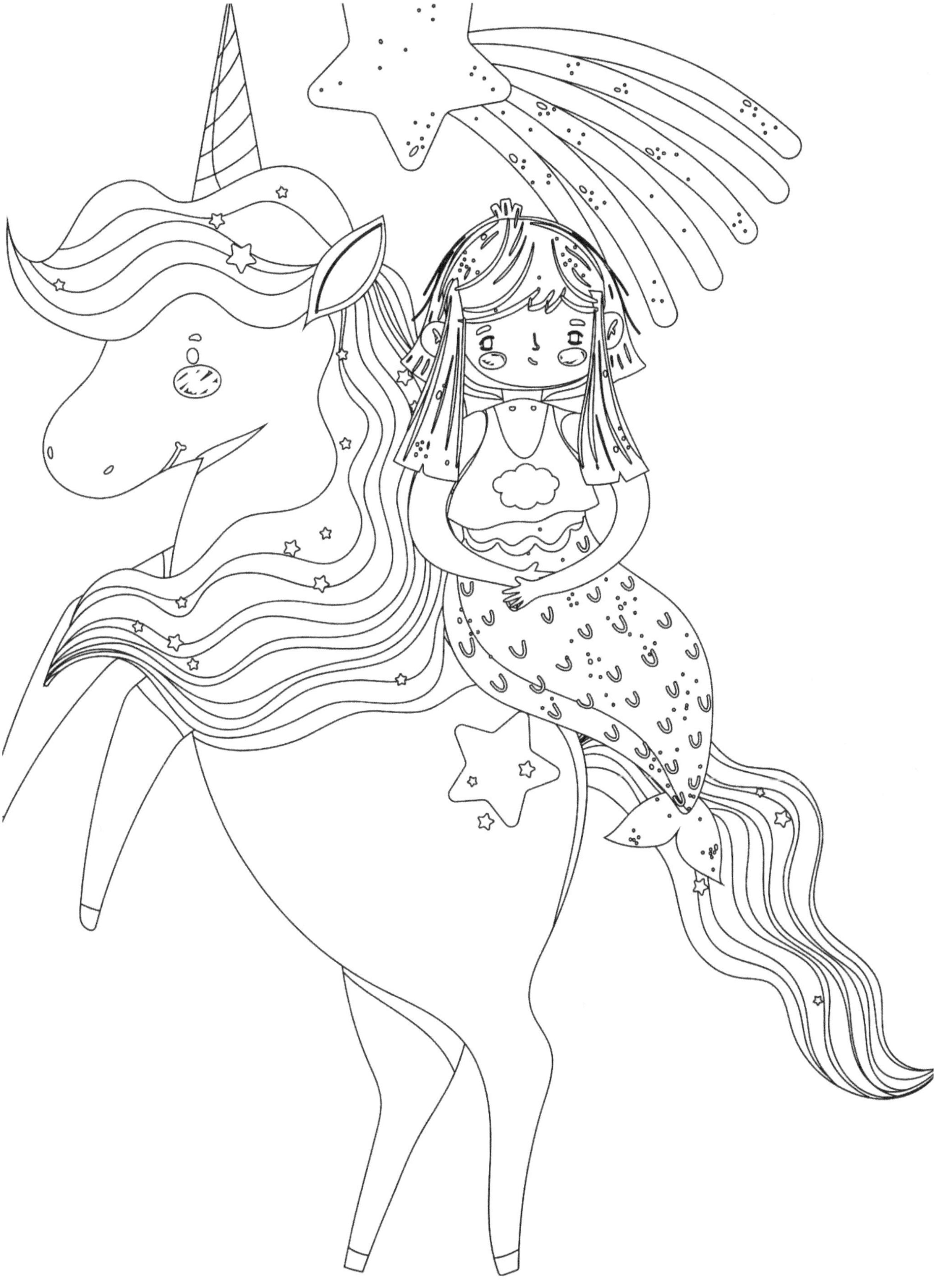

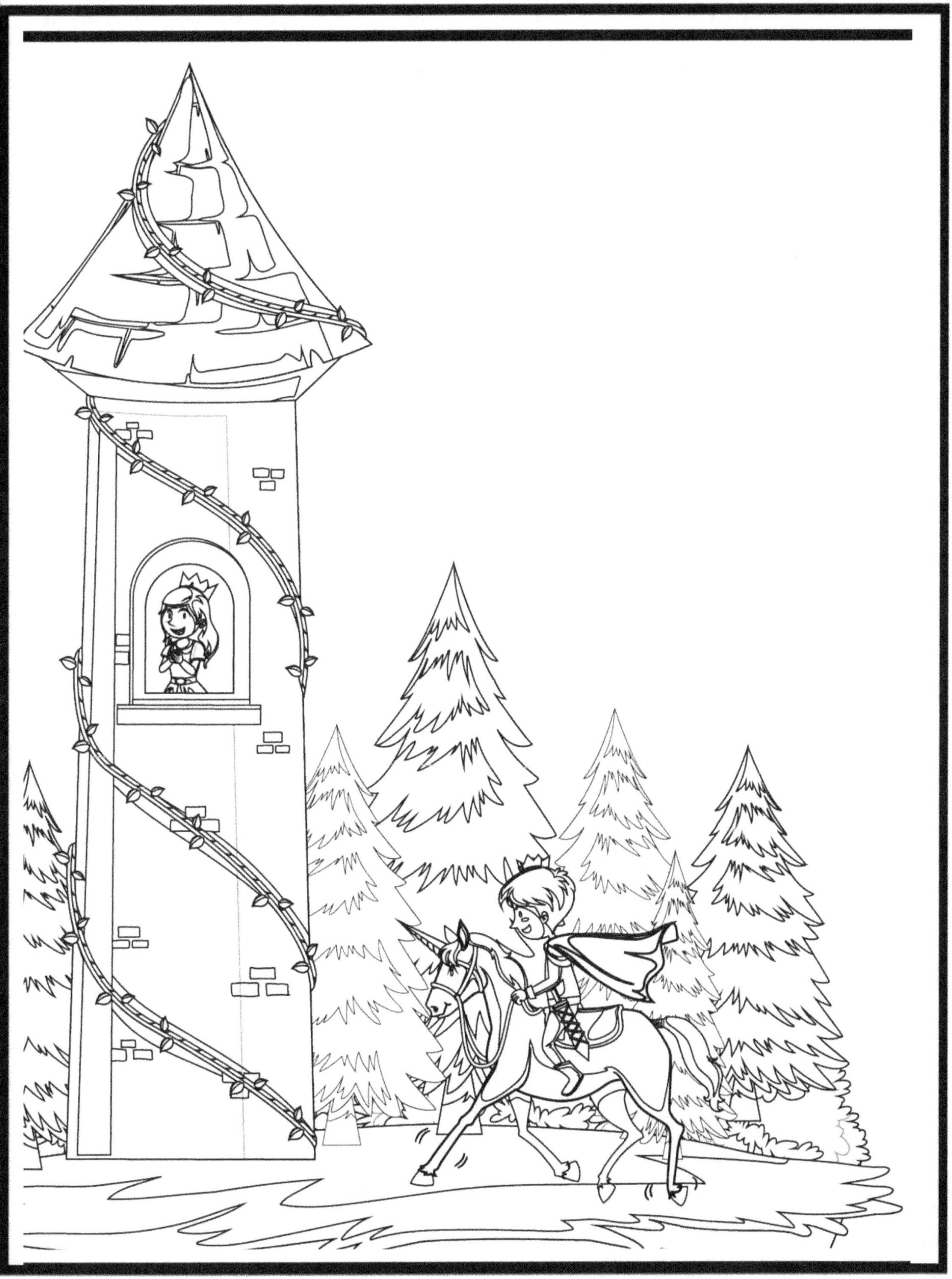

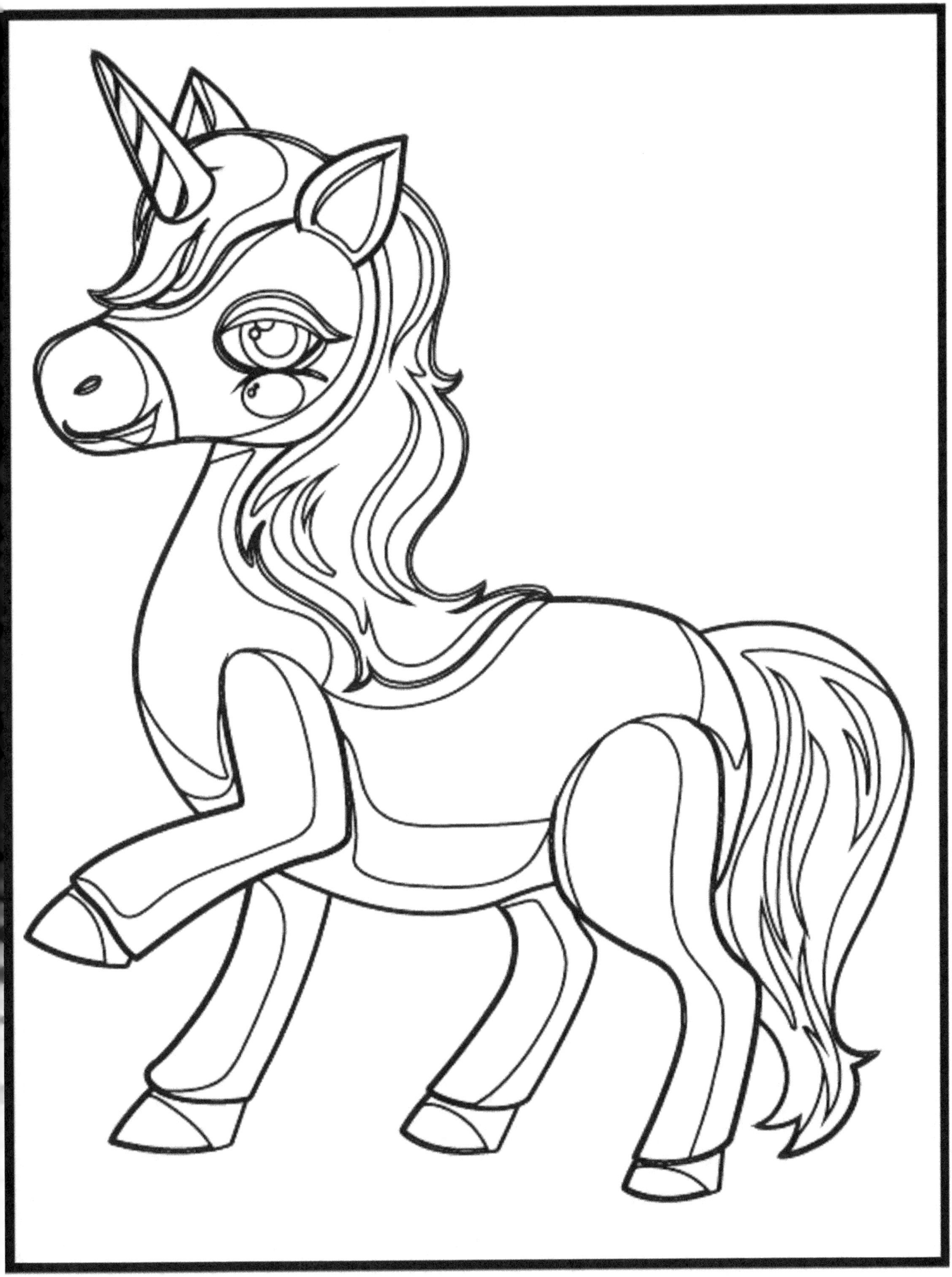

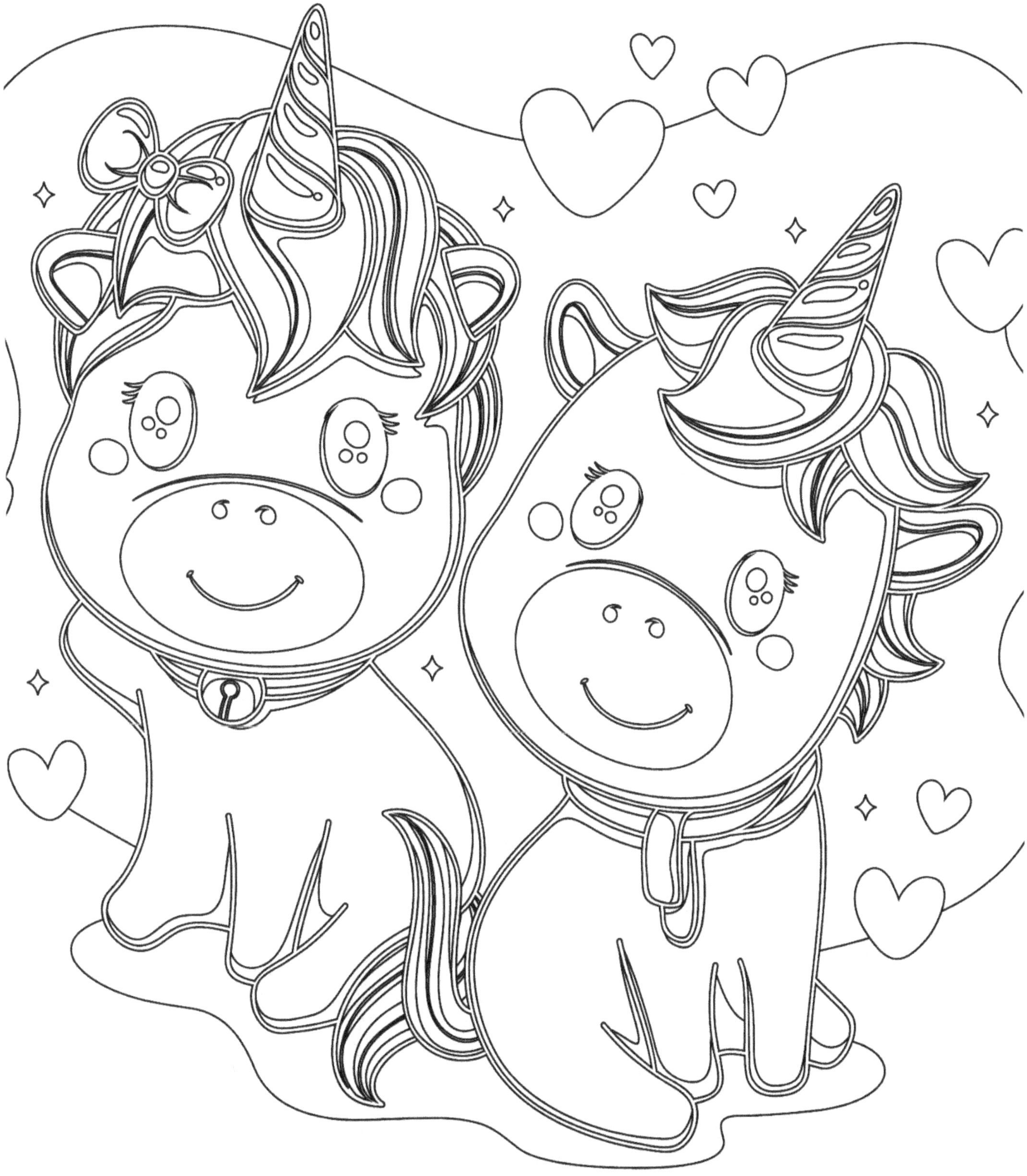

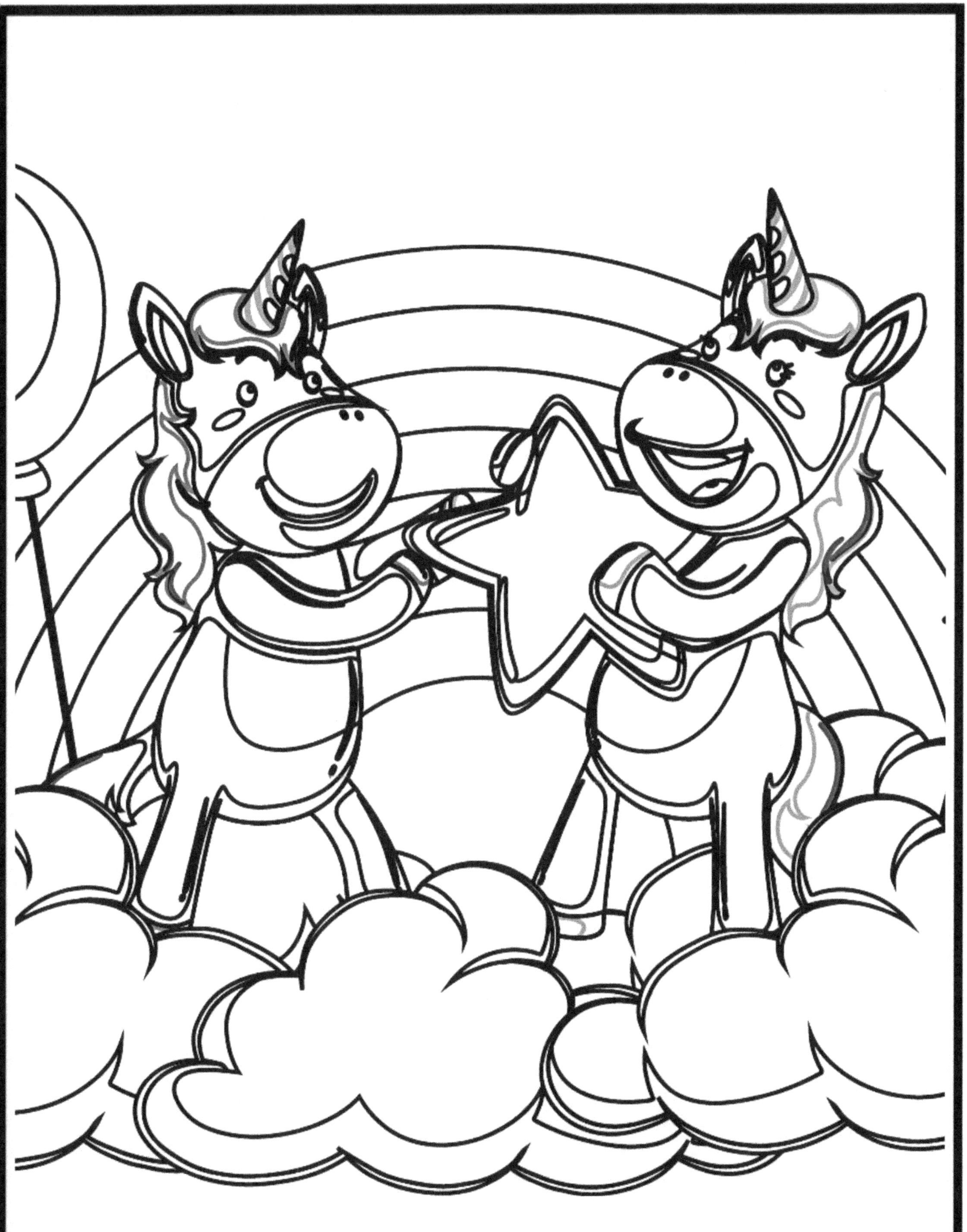

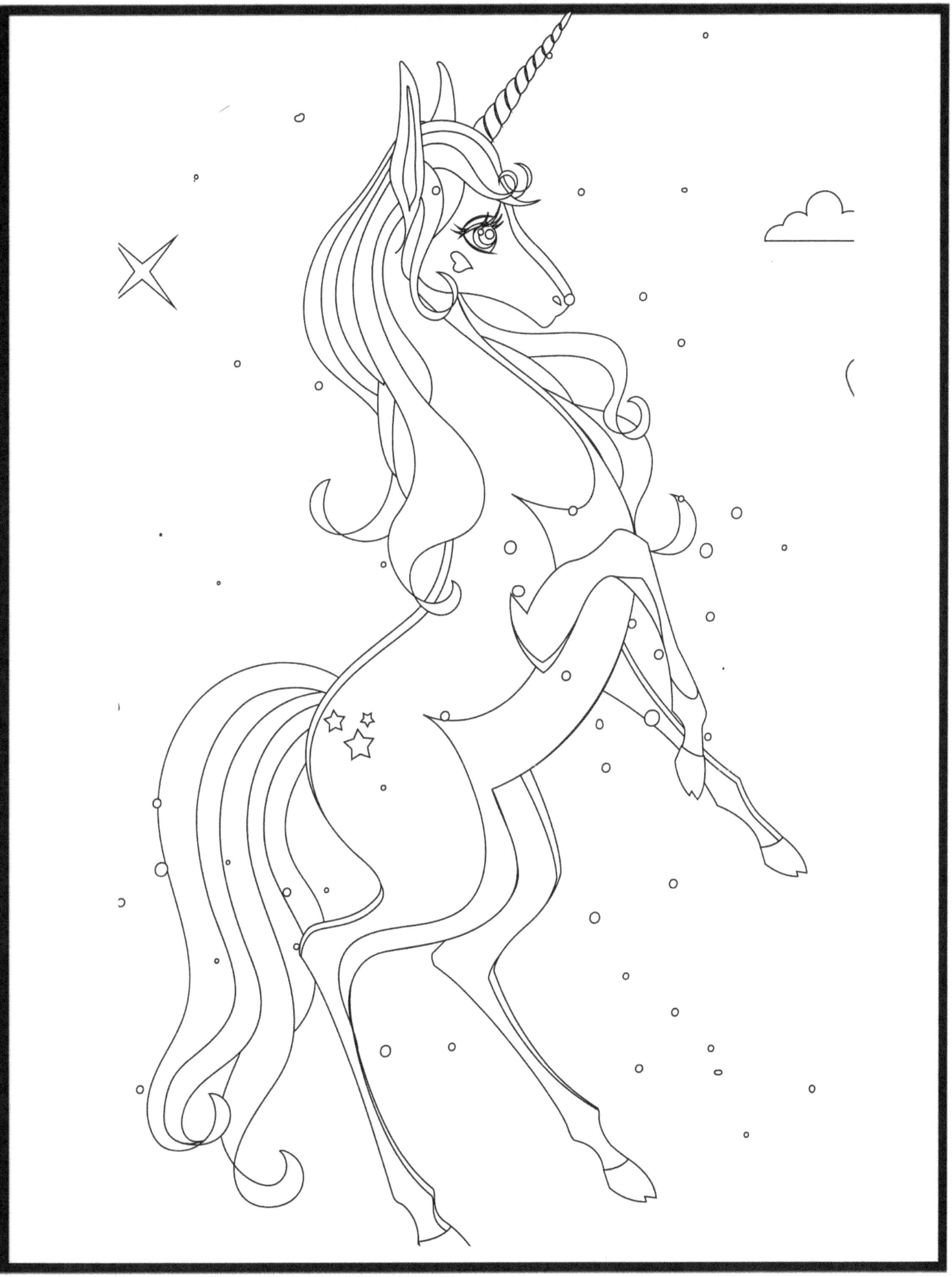

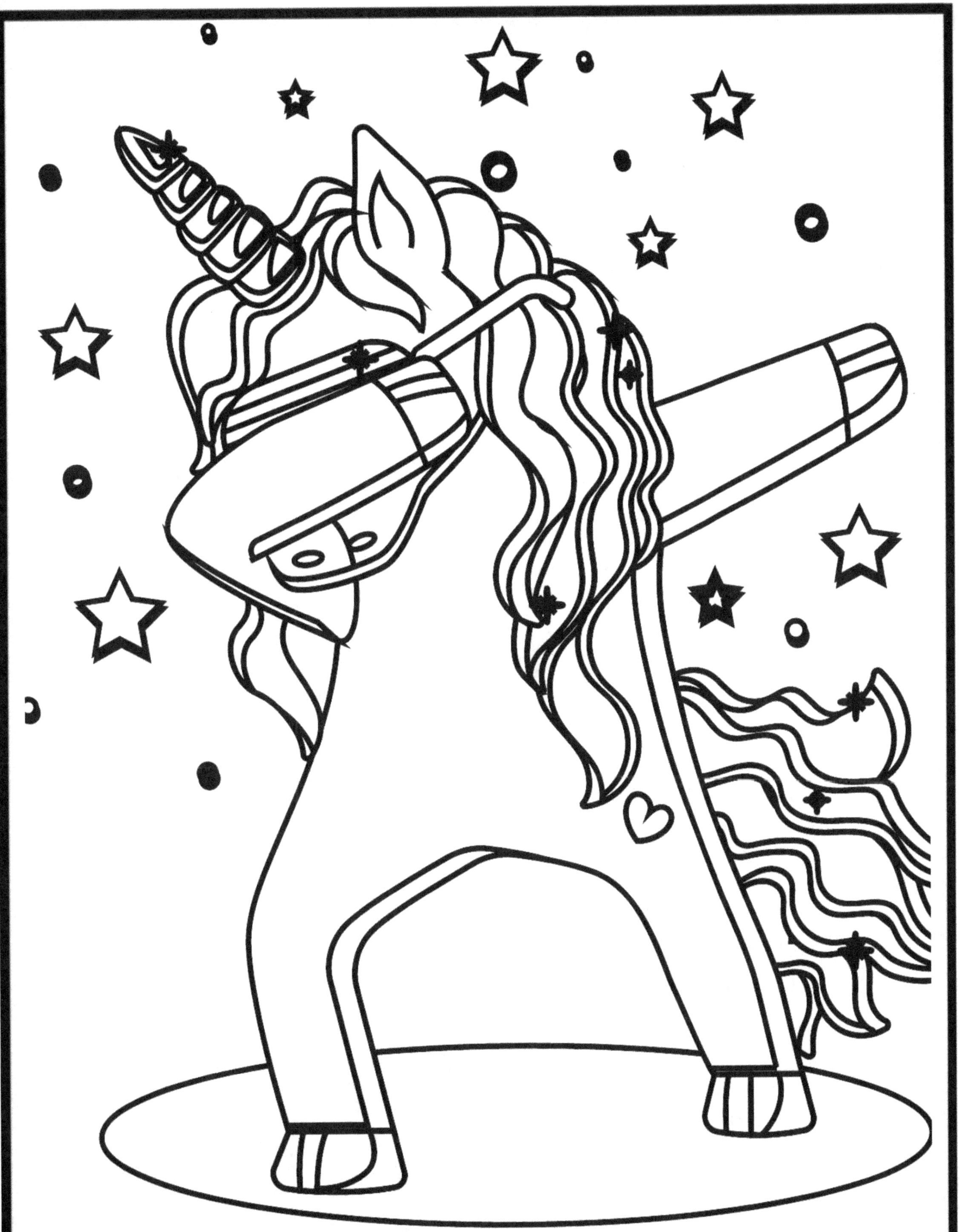

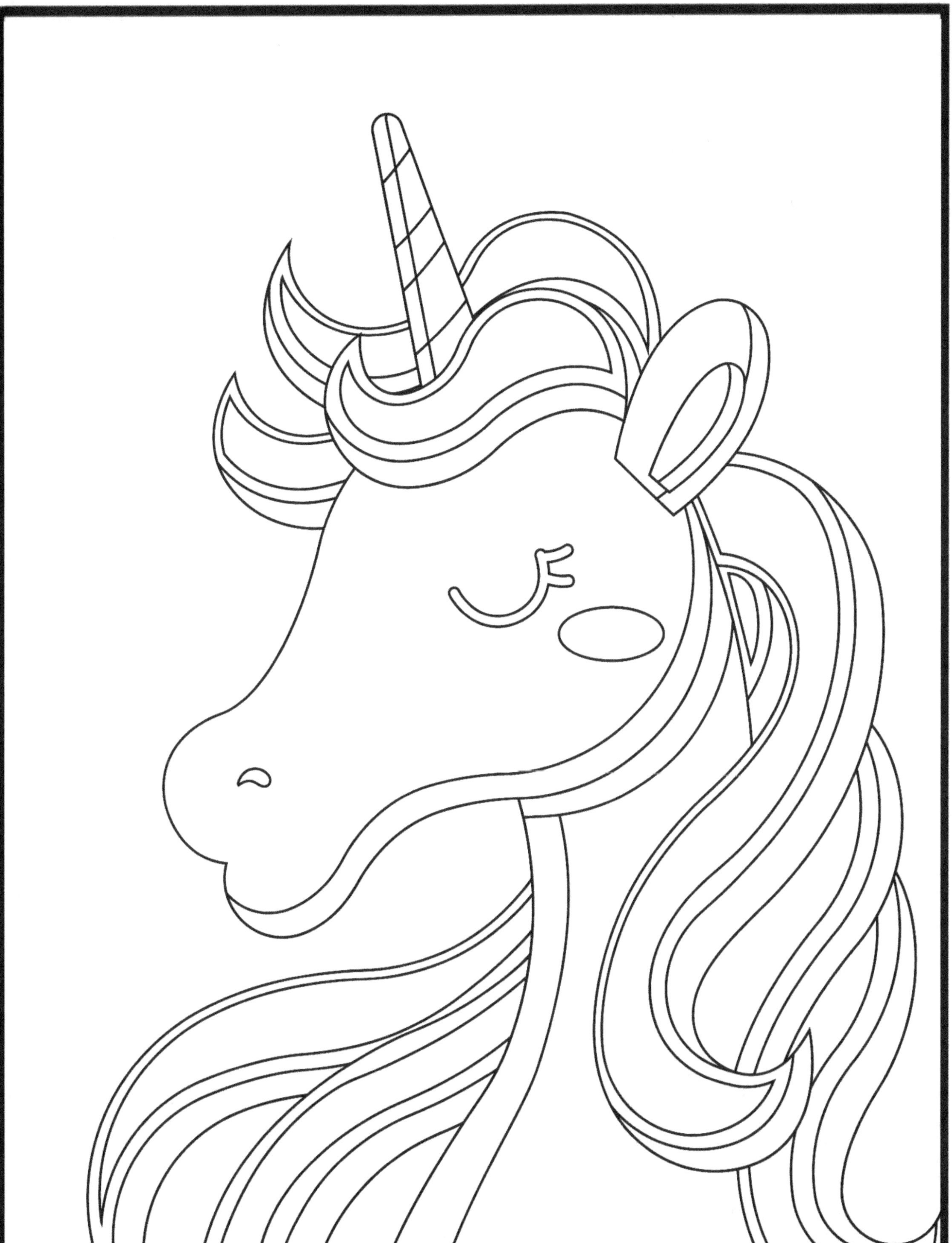

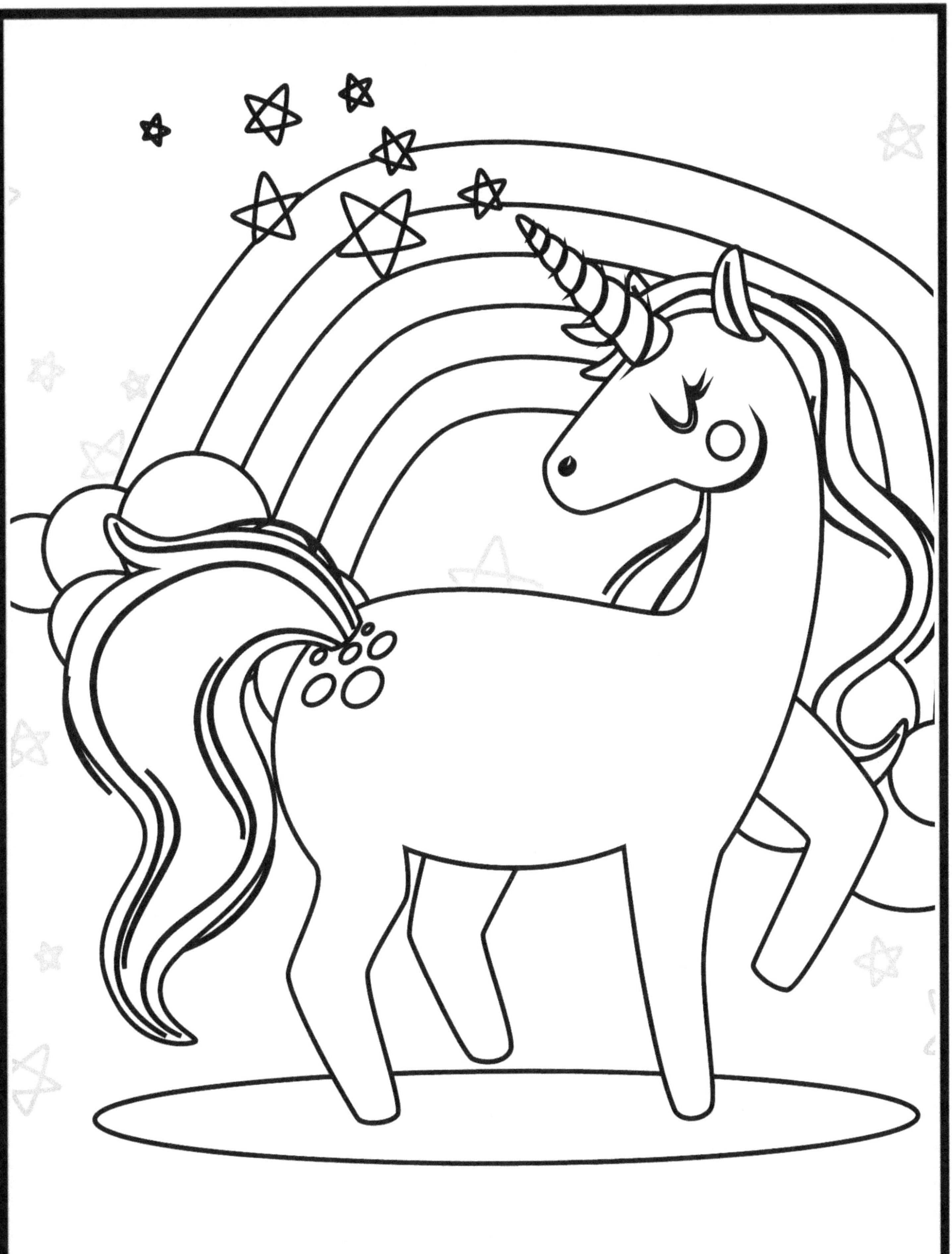

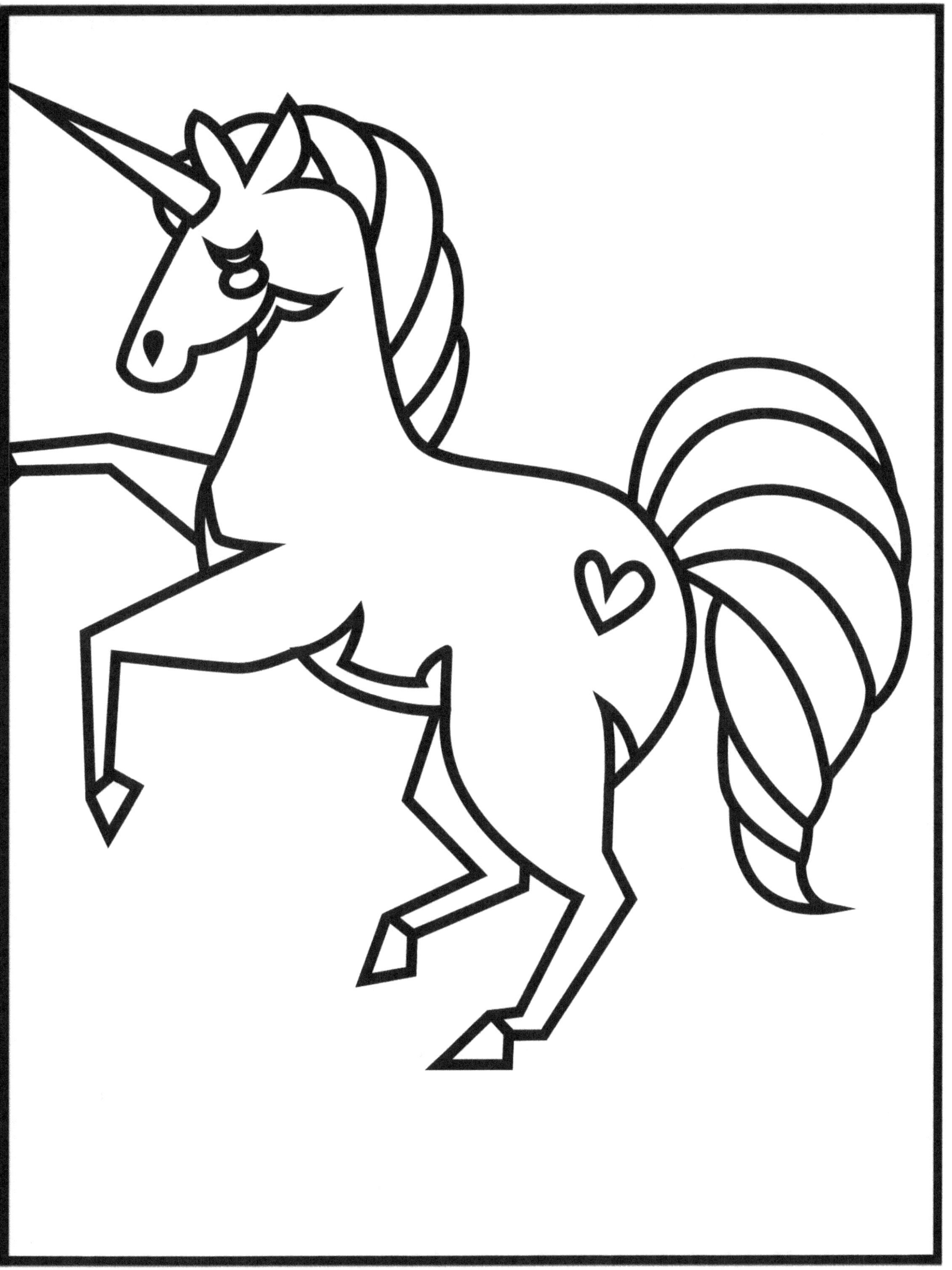

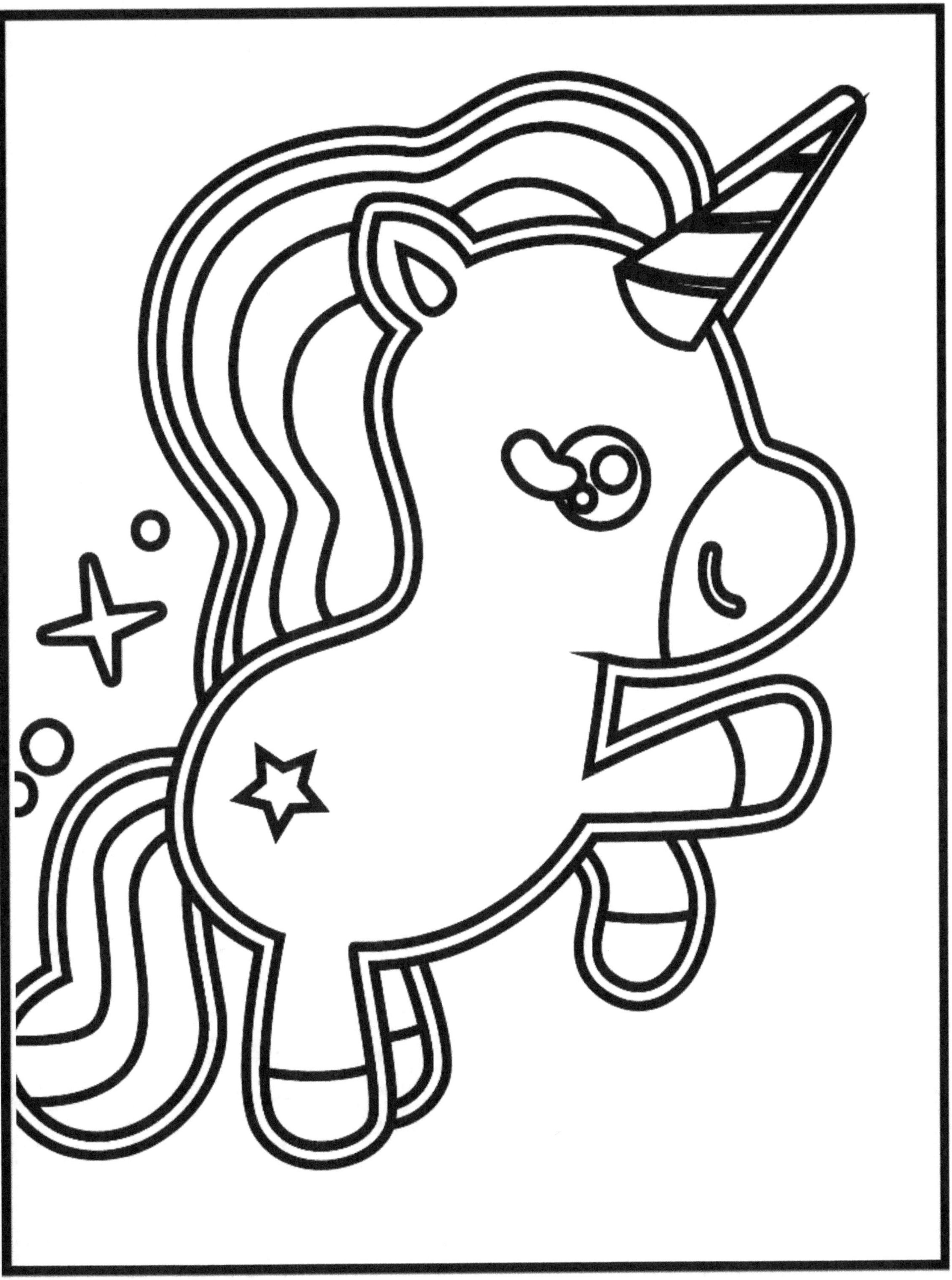

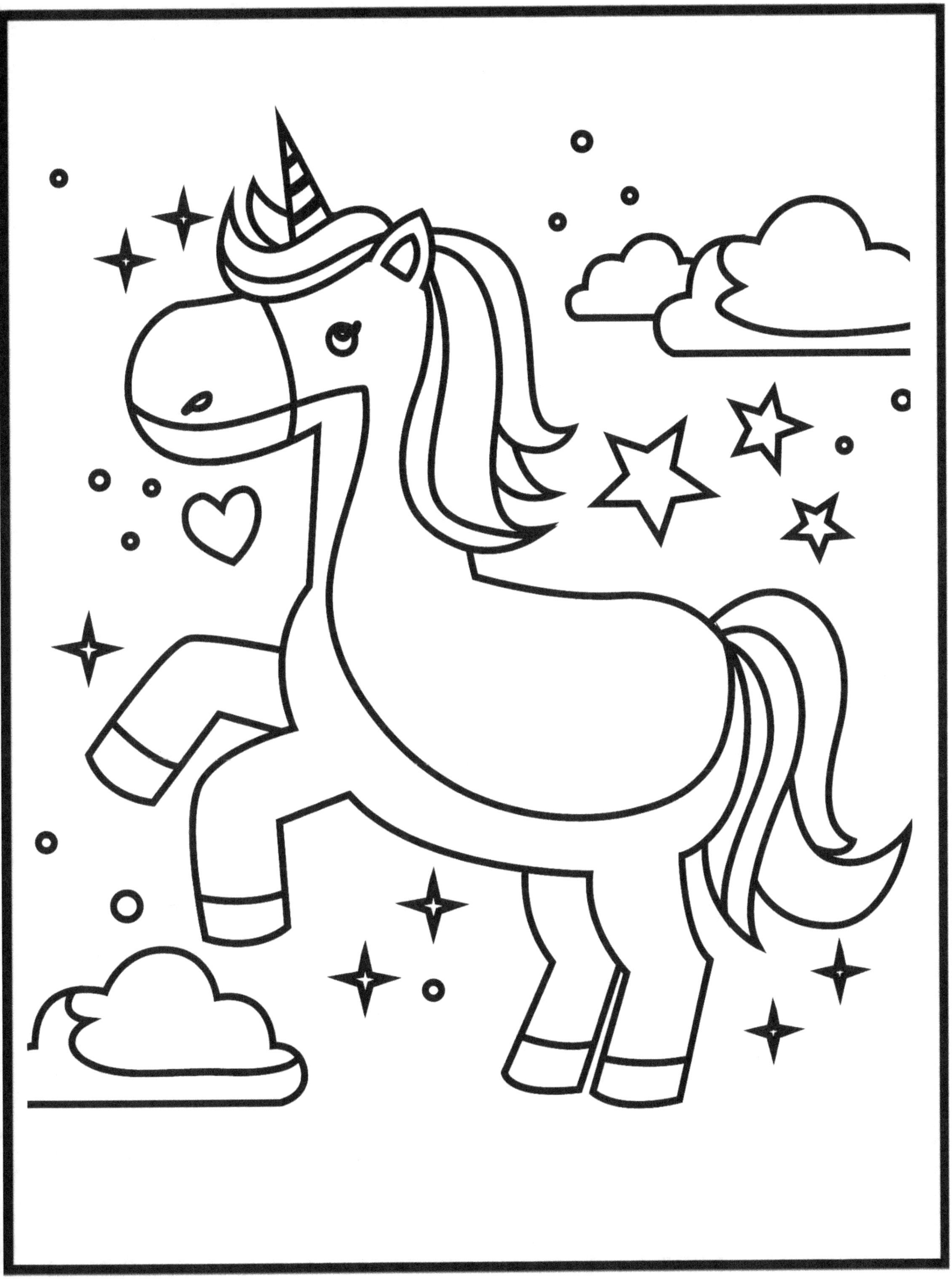

www.ingramcontent.com/pod-product-compliance
Lightning Source LLC
Chambersburg PA
CBHW081058240526
45465CB00025B/2575
9798749768060